Mendes Residence, CA

ORIGINALS

LINDAL CEDAR HOMES

welcome

Few earthly pleasures compare to the ones, great and small, that come

from living in a home of your own design. At Lindal, we've been helping

people craft their dreams of cedar for more than half a century. The ideas

and inspirations we share in these pages are rooted in the lasting strength and beauty of that wondrous wood, a rare commitment to craftsmanship

and the pleasure of helping people transform their fondest dreams into

havens of original beauty and functionality. When it comes to making

your dream come true, we wrote the book. And it's dedicated to you.

table of contents

c o n t

Living in a home of your own design is a deep and daily joy. It's an expression of who you are and how you celebrate life. A renewing refuge

Planning Your Dream

from the outside world. A haven to share with family and friends. Over fifty years and tens of thousands of homes, Lindal Cedar Homes has helped people transform their fondest dreams into original residences of lasting quality, craftsmanship and beauty. We know what it takes to bring a dream to life. As Sherman and Georgia Parks, the homeowners of Deer Parks, have chronicled in the journal that begins on this page, we're with you every step of the way—from your first wish list to the finishing touches.

Deer Parks Journal

JANUARY

It wasn't hard to leave our California condo once we found our 15 acres of paradise in Washougal, Washington— our own forest with a high knoll that's the perfect site for our dream home! We moved in with Georgia's parents during construction. This turned out to be a blessing; her father is a retired master carpenter, and we talked over the day's events with him each night.

Sherman

Continued on page 9.

Lindal's design flexibility makes it easy to create the architectural style you dream of, inside— and out. NJ

"Our home represents a compilation of years spent dreaming of the home we'd were actually able to go ahead and put our ideas on paper for a formal

An unbeatable team
for building a dream:
your dreams and
ideas. Lindal's quality
materials, craftsman-
ship and endless
design possibilities.
And local assistance
from start to finish. WA

build "if" and "when." By the time we

plan, the floorplan just flowed onto the paper." Ian and Holly Green, CT

Every Lindal Cedar
Home is an original.
Our founding philoso-
phy is based on the
belief that the human
spirit is nurtured by
highly personal living
environments that
reflect the passions
and priorities of their
owners. NC

It starts with a desire to build a home as great as all outdoors. A yearning to live every day, not just vacations, by your favorite view. Or a vision to transform a city lot into a very private, very personal urban oasis. Every Lindal begins with a dream—the inspiration to imprint your style on your shelter, to shape your surroundings to your own sense of beauty and functionality, to experience the soul-satisfying rewards of a house that feels like home. So that's

Dreaming

where we encourage you to start—with your dreams. Spend time with them. Get to know them. Above all, don't edit them too early on or discard them as too ambitious. With the help of your design consultant at your local Lindal independent dealership, you'll be surprised how many dreams will come to life as you plan your Lindal original.

Articles and photographs from home magazines are a rich source of advice and inspiration for your Lindal original.

Here's the stuff dreams are made of: our fragrant, fine-grained Western red cedar from the Pacific Northwest. Kiln-dried, cut and planed to a radiant finish at our own sawmill, Lindal cedar is one of nature's most perfect building materials—and a daily luxury to live with. With its natural wonders comes a responsibility; for every Lindal home built, we contribute to forest planting projects to ensure cedar trees for generations to come.

"Our dealer was involved every step of the way." Pam Jackson, ON

Perhaps your dream begins with your own piece of earthly paradise—and the desire for a dwelling that reflects the natural beauty of your site.

A wish list may be the first time you put your dreams down on paper. It's an easy way to shift your creativity into high gear—and a helpful point of reference as you share your ideas with your local Lindal consultant.

The answer to a dream: the Burrows residence in Ontario, with its idyllic waterfront setting—and views that stretch for miles. ON

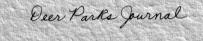

Deer Parks Journal

JANUARY

Sherman chose Lindal for cedar's resistance to pests and dry rot. I chose it for the utter beauty of Lindal cedar and the freedom to design our dream. Both of us are inspired by the cedar beach cabin that my father built in the 1960s. It's as beautiful today as the day it was built, with very little maintenance over those 30-plus years. With a track record like that—and a track record like Lindal's—how could we go wrong?

Georgia

Continued on page 16

Western red cedar was the source of great healing and spiritual meaning for Native Americans, who addressed it as "Long Life Maker" and "Life Giver."

Planning your Lindal
original begins right
here, with the ideas
in this book. You may
want to use one of
the proven home
plans in our design
library as a point of
departure, making
changes and modifi-
cations according to
your wants and needs.

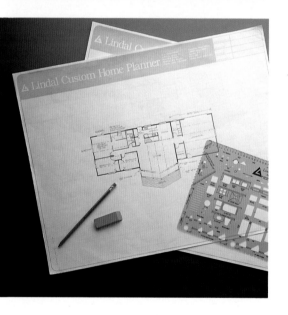

Transforming your dream into a working design is one of the greatest challenges of creating an original home. It's also one of the reasons why

From Dream to Design

people choose Lindal—and their local Lindal dealership. According to Dick and Jo Feroe of Smith Mountain Lake, Virginia, "Roland and Betty Riddick did more than sell us a house; we must have visited them a dozen times before we had our final plans. They drew, redrew, figured and refigured, helping us every step of the way. Their honesty, integrity and personal warmth have made them not just people we admire, but personal friends as well." The Feroe home is featured on pages 114-115.

If you enjoy the
design process and
want to do most of it
yourself, our Home
Planning Kit is an
invaluable resource.
So is your Lindal
consultant, who
will work with you
from your first wish
list to your final plan.

Create your own
Lindal home from
the ground up, as a
growing number of
Lindal homeowners
do. If you work with
architects, we're
happy to work with
them, too. ON

"We were able to create our plan according to our priorities." Derek and Candy Stott, ON

Your Lindal consultant sends your plans to our Engineering Department, where time-honored draftsmanship works hand-in-hand with Computer-Aided Design (CAD) systems to produce your blueprints.

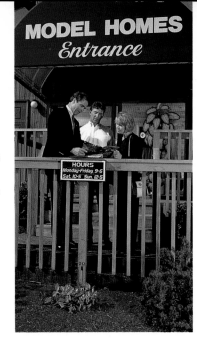

Your local Lindal consultant can help you make the most of your building site, provide design assistance, analyze your plan's feasibility and cost, and help oversee your order through delivery—and beyond.

"Our Lindal consultant's insights have been responsible in many ways for our complete satisfaction with the design of our new home." Greg and Lydia LaHaie, OR

MA

Making plans means making choices—and when you're planning a Lindal original, the options are infinite. Lindal's architectural flexibility and beauty begin with our two major building systems: Cedar Frame and Solid Cedar. Our Cedar Frame system gives you a choice of three exterior looks, which run the spectrum from sleek and contemporary to  rich and rustic. Whatever building system you choose, your personal design choices open up even further inside, thanks to the flexibility of Lindal's time-proven post and beam architecture, the legacy of North American master builders. This strong framework frees the interior walls from bearing any structural load, so your imagination is virtually the only limit to your floorplan.

Cedar Frame with Classic tongue and groove cedar siding, usually placed vertically.

Cedar Frame with Clap-board cedar siding—overlapping boards placed horizontally.

Cedar Frame with Round Log siding, horizontally placed. Optional stockade corners.

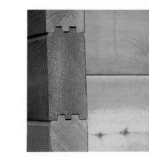

Solid Cedar. Single wall, solid wood building system, sturdily constructed of four-inch-thick interlocking cedar timbers. Dovetail corners.

Cedar Frame
• Double wall, frame construction.
• Outside, your choice of three exterior siding options covers the wall system with an R-22 rating.
• Roof system is frame R-33.
• More information on pages 252–253.

Solid Cedar
• Single wall, solid wood construction.
• Outside walls constructed of solid 4x8 cedar timbers for thermal mass and high energy efficiency.
• Roof system is rigid insulation R-38.
• More information on pages 254–255.

"We would have a hard time living in a "normal" house again. We enjoy the open feeling and appreciate the flexibility of design inherent in post and beam construction." Frank Godfrey, ON

The ability to grow and change, unencumbered by structural constraints, is another strength of post and beam construction; it's easy to take out interior walls or add a wing.

Post and beam architecture is the key to your Lindal's design flexibility. The roof's weight is supported by a strong framework of posts and beams, instead of the interior walls on which conventional construction depends. RI

Western red cedar
is beautiful all by
itself—or enhanced
by accents of other
natural building
materials.

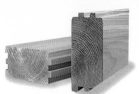

Accent with stone . . .

or brick . . .

or stucco.

Endless Possibilities

The magic of planning your dream really comes home in Lindal's infinite

possibilities for design, style, size, floor plans and energy-efficient living

in any climate or terrain. Whatever elements of style you choose, you can

count on the lasting quality, craftsmanship and value that have distin-

guished Lindal Cedar Homes for half a century.

Local stone comple-
ments the cedar. ON

You can build a
small treasure in
less than 1000
square feet. WA

Or celebrate life
on a grand scale
of 5000 square
feet or more. NC

"What we like best is our home's natural elegance, created by the combination of wood, stone and glass, and

Put any roof on
any plan. CT

Go for a sleek,
modern interior. SC

Bring the beauty of
cedar inside. TN

Bring the outdoors in
with a sunroom. VA

Triumph over a
sloping site. VT

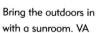

Whatever your climate, Lindal can engineer for snow, wind and seismic requirements—and your hot tub! ID

A Lindal is warm, snug and energy efficient on the coldest, snowiest day in the mountains. CA

In the tropics a Lindal combats heat and humidity, insects and pests, and welcomes tradewinds. HI

a year~round feeling of being in contact with nature." Heinz and Lisa Heller, TN

Make the most of your view. ID

Create a desert oasis. TX

Community or commercial too. CT

Build anywhere in the world. Japan

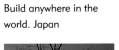

Most Lindal homeowners are not intimately involved in the day-to-day,

hands-on construction of their home. Others, like the family featured in

Building: A Labor of Love

our journal, wouldn't have it any other way. But whether you follow

your builder's progress from a distance or are in the trenches hammering

every nail yourself, you'll appreciate all the things we do, large and small,

to make the entire process go as smoothly as is humanly possible. Our

fifty years' experience in helping people build their dream homes is at

your disposal. And so is the service of your Lindal dealership—locally

owned and independently operated.

Deer Parks Journal

JANUARY–MARCH

With the help of her parents and our
Lindal consultant, Ole Rasmussen,
Georgia planned our solid cedar home.
(I handled the technical and business
aspects of things.) Ole is working closely
with us and our ideas. He measured
and drew up our plot plan and the plans
for the structural specifications. He
arranged for us to meet other Lindal
owners, who gave us great ideas!
He's even helping us get our bank loan
(facilitated by Lindal's good name).

Sherman

Continued on page 76

We've been antici-
pating builders'
needs for fifty years,
developing ways to
make the job go
smoothly from start
to finish.

Final blueprints are
keyed to the number-
ing system on your
building components
and materials list, so
it's quick and easy to
find what you need.

"The high quality of Lindal's materials seemed

When materials run late, so do builders. We help prevent these construction headaches by delivering all Lindal building materials in one convenient shipment (or more, if desirable).

We're so confident of every Lindal home's lasting quality that we guarantee it; our ten-year warranty is the best in the industry.

to bring out the best in the construction crews." Rick and Angie Smith, ON

The expertise behind the scenes: your Lindal consultant can help you with local building regulations and zoning, and can assist you in finding reputable builders, contractors and subs —even help secure financing, insurance and building permits.

inspirations

Every Lindal cedar home is an original. Most have roots in our design

library. But a growing number of Lindals are inspired, from the ground

up, by the singular visions and lifestyles of their owners. So if your

notion of a dream home is one that you or your architect designs, you're in good company, as you can see from the homes in this chapter. What's

more, you don't pay a premium for the luxury of designing your own

Lindal original. A modest design fee, based on the square footage of your

home, is all it takes to transform your inspirations into working plans

and final blueprints.

With cedar siding, stucco accents and a tile roof, our "cover" home does

full justice to its panoramic setting on Lake Norman. Designed around a

love for outdoor activities and entertaining, the home of Marshall and

Casa Islena

Frances Digh takes advantage of every opportunity to open out to views and alfresco settings on the

surrounding lakefront. All this luxury has its practical side; the Dighs'

local Lindal consultant worked with them to ensure a lifetime of low

maintenance and energy costs.

The Digh Residence

Bedrooms: 4 + Office + Library + Studio + Bonus Room

Bathrooms: 3 Full +1 Three-quarter + 1 Half

Master bedroom on first floor

Total Area: 6742 sq. ft.

First Floor: 3962 sq. ft.

Other Floor: 2780 sq. ft.

Size: 116' x 74'

Entry: Front

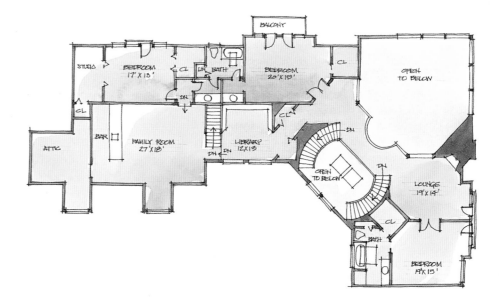

Please note:

Dimensions on all Inspirations

chapter plans are rounded up

and down to the closest foot.

Casa Islena (Island House) is a lake-front landmark—and winner of the North Carolina Home Builders Grand Award for Design.

A sunroom enhances the master bedroom—and captures the view.

Lavishly used throughout the home, Italian marble adds a feeling of elegance and luxury to the master bathroom.

"We love cedar, and thought cedar and stucco together would give our home a flair that would be unique to our area." Frances Digh, NC

The plan is centered around a stunning great room with two 27-foot-high glass walls and a two-story stone fireplace.

"Our designer, West Eppley (of Carolina Custom Homes) was most helpful. He took my two pages of requests and created this beautiful design." Frances Digh, NC

A view through the living room to Lake Norman is framed by two custom circular staircases in oak.

Bleached cedar timbers give this Washington home a clean, contemporary look that's a world apart from the typical log home.

An Enlightened Log Home

If you've ever thought you'd have to sacrifice a light, modern look to get

the natural wonders of a log home, take a look at this solid cedar Lindal.

Its owners combined the best of current architecture with solid cedar

construction to create a home with a sure sense of contemporary style.

Bleached cedar adds light and a modern sensibility that's in keeping with

the home's island setting.

An Enlightened Log Home
Bedrooms: 2 + Den
Bathrooms: 2 Full
Total Area: 2490 sq. ft.
Size: 99' x 50'
Entry: Front

The structure of the roof beams gives style as well as strength.

This solid cedar Lindal home embraces a terrace with a spectacular view of Puget Sound.

"I had my own design and was pleased that Lindal could prepare drawings and specs adaptable to my plan." Homeowner, WA

The attention to detail and drama is evident from the inviting entrance of this Lindal original. Another view is shown on page 130.

Making the most of their spectacular valley view was the inspiration for Jeff and Connie Conrad as they designed their Lindal home in California. "Lindal's post and beam construction provides for the most viewing potential. The energy-efficient windows allowed us to exploit our valley view and capture the Western sunsets while maintaining compliance with all local building regulations." With beautiful results, we might add.

Modern Outlook

The Conrad Residence
Bedrooms: 3
Bathrooms: 2 Full + 1 Half
Master bedroom on second floor
Total Area: 2505 sq. ft.
First Floor: 1242 sq. ft.
Other Floor: 1263 sq. ft.
Size: 65' x 40'
Entry: Side

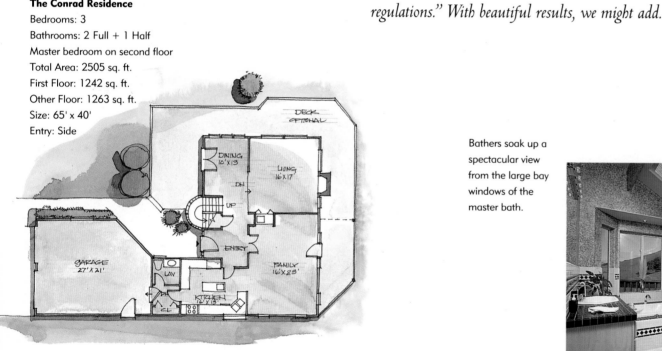

Bathers soak up a spectacular view from the large bay windows of the master bath.

The master bedroom's open airiness is enhanced by high ceilings and French doors that lead out to a second-floor balcony.

"We would recommend a Lindal home for anyone owning view property." Jeff and Connie Conrad, CA

"Lindal gave us the flexibility to have both a traditional kitchen and family room with exposed beams, along with a dramatically contemporary living room featuring marble and vaulted ceilings just steps away."

Stone House Revival

The Welches' letter says it all: "Our Lindal was an addition to an existing home that I purchased from my great uncle's estate. The original house was a 40-year-old stone ranch house with a dormer in the back. I believe the original house was about 1,200 square feet. It is now 4,755 square feet. So it ended up being quite an addition."

"Wayne and Anita South of Cedar Classics contacted us when they heard we were working on an addition. Your catalog, along with Wayne and Anita's endorsement, went a long way to convince us that a Lindal addition was a perfect match to our stone house. They certainly were correct.

It is now a home with plenty of space, yet everyone feels comfortable. They say 'it's homey.' That's a nice comment, one you do not often get for a large home. So what do we like best? I guess the answer is the warmth.

Is it energy efficient? Truthfully, it seems to cost me less money than the 1,800-square-foot house I previously owned.

Did we design our dream home? Absolutely. With Wayne and the architect's help, we were able to build what I call 'a man's dream.'

I was very worried when I started this project that I would mess up what was already a beautiful stone house. Instead, we created the 'dream house' my wife and I had always wanted.

I would recommend both Lindal Cedar Homes and Cedar Classics to anyone who asks, and many have!"

Scott Welch   Henrietta A. Welch

Scott and Henrietta Welch
N.W. New Jersey

The spacious sun-room off the kitchen opens up living to the great outdoors.

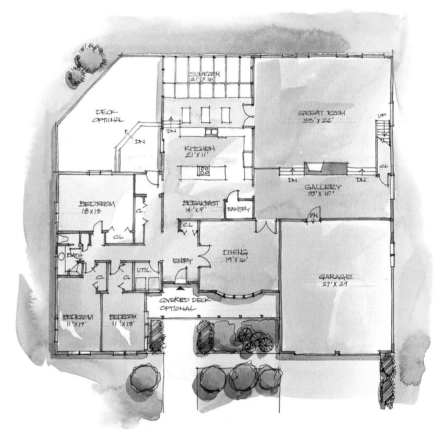

A covered veranda is both cozy and inviting.

The Welch Residence

Bedrooms: 4 + Sitting Room
Bathrooms: 1 Full + 1 Three-quarter + 1 Half
Master bedroom on second floor
Total Area: 4755 sq. ft.
First Floor: 3359 sq. ft.
Other Floor: 1396 sq. ft.
Size: 79' x 66'
Entry: Front

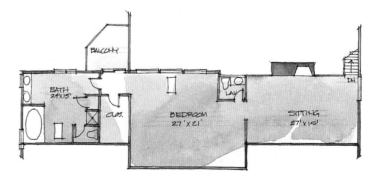

The front of the Welch home is graced with local stone—and complemented by cedar clapboard on the other three sides.

Timeless Treasures

How can a new home accommodate its owners' longings for a stone fire-place, bay windows and furniture with a past? Beautifully—when it's a Lindal. Yvonne and Sam Shantz of Ontario, Canada, wanted "not a modern home, but a country home in which we could use the furniture collected through the years." And they got it—by designing a Lindal that brings the warmth and beauty of finely finished Western red cedar inside, on interior walls, ceilings and trim.

Cedar trim complements the living room's stone fireplace and traditional furnishings.

Hardwood floors, custom cabinetry and a cedar-lined ceiling keep the modern kitchen in style with the rest of the house; an astral window echoes the roofline and adds light to the rich wood interior.

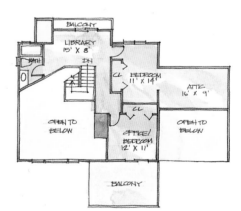

The Shantz Residence

Bedrooms: 3 + Library + Bonus Room

Bathrooms: 2 Full + 2 Half

Master bedroom on first floor

Total Area: 2398 sq. ft.

First Floor: 1714 sq. ft.

Other Floor: 684 sq. ft.

Size: 64' x 34'

Entry: Back

"Our local Lindal consultant was very helpful. We worked together on the plans for our home."

Northwest Light

Lanny and Sherry Dusek wanted a Lindal home that would let in the

soft "oyster" light and natural beauty of its site in Kelso, Washington.

Working closely with their local Lindal consultant, they designed a home

that combines an unerring sense of dramatic style with the functionality

so important to a working couple and two teenage daughters.

Wanting to be good
neighbors, the Duseks
designed the front
facade to blend with
the neighborhood.
Cedar clapboard was
their preference.

The Dusek Residence
Bedrooms: 3 + Office
Bathrooms: 3 Full + 1 Half
Master bedroom on first floor
Total Area: 2765 sq. ft.
First Floor: 1815 sq. ft.
Other Floor: 950 sq. ft.
Size: 67' x 34'
Entry: Front

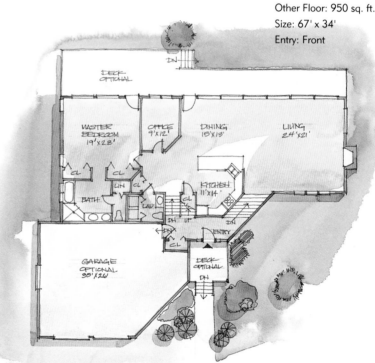

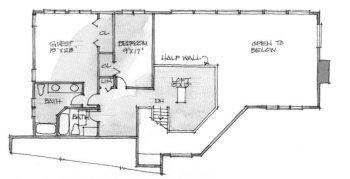

"We enjoy the open-
ness of our home.
The generous win-
dows form an almost
transparent barrier
between the inside
and out."

Neighborly by Design

With the help of their local Lindal dealership and contractor, LaVern and Franklin Skala designed a cedar clapboard Lindal that fits beautifully into their neighborhood in Greenville, South Carolina. "We all worked together as a team and it paid off in the end," LaVern says. "We now have our Lindal Dream Home."

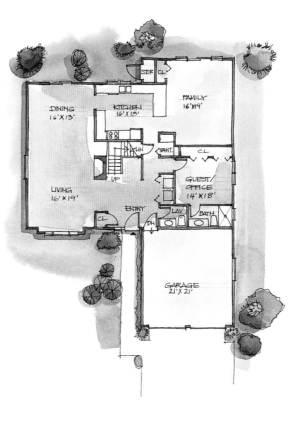

The Skala Residence
Bedrooms: 4
Bathrooms: 2 Full + 1 Three-quarter + 1 Half
Master bedroom on second floor
Total Area: 2572 sq. ft.
First Floor: 1661 sq. ft.
Other Floor: 911 sq. ft.
Size: 48' x 59'
Entry: Front

Dream Ranch

Situated among the celebrity homesteads in California's Santa Ynez country, this sweeping ranch home was designed to suit the owners' casual lifestyle and take in the spectacular views from its prime hilltop location. In a design that echoes the open grandeur of the surrounding ranchland, every room in the house looks out to rolling hills and wild oak—a picturesque setting that's home to horses and llamas.

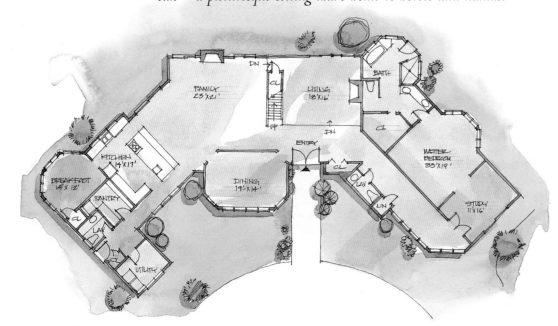

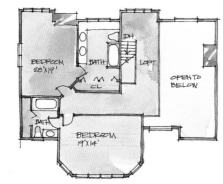

Dream Ranch
Bedrooms: 3 + Study
Bathrooms: 3 Full + 2 Half
Master bedroom on first floor
Total Area: 4165 sq. ft.
First Floor: 3180 sq. ft.
Other Floor: 985 sq. ft.
Size: 111' x 58'
Entry: Front

This Lindal original takes full advantage of its post and beam construction to create an open, airy interior —enhanced by the living room's two-story ceiling.

The master bedroom suite occupies its own wing of the house, complete with sumptuous bath and adjacent study.

Making the most of a site: This cedar clapboard Lindal was designed to be at home on its hill overlooking the Santa Ynez ranchlands.

The library gets its own lofty location—a book-lover's dream.

After fifteen years of making getaways to their "farm" in Slatington,

Pennsylvania, the Smith family turned their weekend retreat into a full-

Pine Hill Farm

time dream come true. With the help of their Lindal consultant, they

designed a home that fits their lifestyle, lives in harmony with its rural set-

ting—and takes full advantage of the panoramic views that surround them.

"The great room is curved to blend with the curvature of a hill that slopes away from the front of the house."

The Smith Residence
Bedrooms: 3 + Library/Office
Bathrooms: 2 + 1 Half
Master bedroom on second floor
Total Area: 2979 sq. ft.
First Floor: 2123 sq. ft.
Other Floor: 856 sq. ft.
Size: 70' x 51'
Entry: Front

"At the end of a business day, it is good to come home. We feel that living in our house is like living in a dream come true."

"This is a house made for music, not TV." Mrs. Smith, PA

"Our house is a striking combination of the beauty of cedar and the interest of its many lines and angles."

"During construction, it was exciting to see the pictures in our minds, our ideas, become a reality."

Holly and Ian Green wanted their Lindal home to live in harmony with the surrounding landscape and wildlife on their Connecticut property. With the help of their Lindal dealership, they created "a structure that just # Woodland Retreat

seems to belong in its woodland setting," Holly says. "It seems at peace with nature. I love the expanses of cedar, glass and stone. The feeling is completely airy and open—it suits our lifestyle. It's great for entertaining—inside and out!"

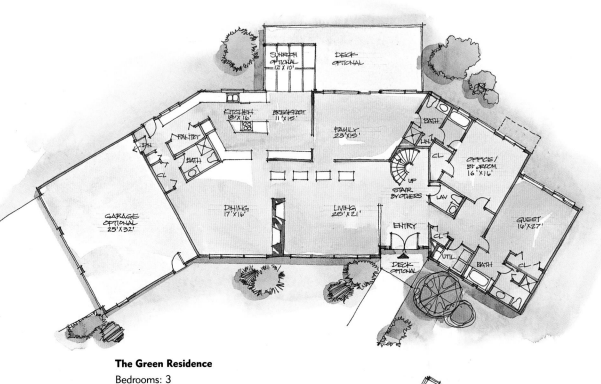

The sunroom provides a tranquil retreat just off the breakfast area and adjoining deck. According to Holly, "the wood frames are always comfortable to the touch, unlike metal frames in other homes."

The Green Residence
Bedrooms: 3
Bathrooms: 3 Full + 1 Three-quarter + 1 Half
Master bedroom on second floor
Total Area: 3804 sq. ft.
First Floor: 3256 sq. ft.
Other Floor: 548 sq. ft.
Size: 104' x 50'
Entry: Front

The Greens designed their Lindal original with its natural setting well in mind.

A multi-level deck wraps around the front of the LaHaie home, providing a spacious place for outdoor entertaining—and a sweeping view from the 2.5-acre hilltop site in Hillsboro, Oregon.

Hilltop Oasis

"We dreamed of a home where the beauty of wood would surround us!" write Greg and Lydia LaHaie. Taking advantage of the view was another priority. *"Our dealer built a scale model of our plan; he was extremely supportive in every detail of our dealings. His insights have been responsible in many ways for our complete satisfaction with the design of our new home."*

The foundation of a dream: Greg and Lydia photographed this unique triptych of their home's beginnings.

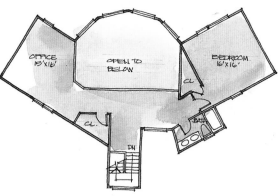

The LaHaie Residence
Bedrooms: 2 + Office
Bathrooms: 2 Full + 2 Half
Master bedroom on first floor
Total Area: 2832 sq. ft.
First Floor: 1939 sq. ft.
Other Floor: 893 sq. ft.
Size: 84' x 40'
Entry: Front

"Lindal's design professionals turned an architect's concept into our one-of-a-kind dream home come true."

"We found all the components of our Lindal home were of breathtaking quality, from the beams and wood windows to the siding and French doors." Greg and Lydia LaHaie, OR

Stairs wrap around a cylindrical tower to the observatory. MA

A lofty lookout off a main deck.

You'll be glad to know that Lindal gives you true creative license to design the home of your dreams. You're in control—and we're here to help you take full advantage of all the freedom and flexibility you deserve. As you

Anything Goes

can see throughout this book, the independent spirit of our customers—and their homes—comes through in every Lindal. Many of the features are standard, others are optional— and still others are homebuyer innovations that they're kindly sharing.

A spiral staircase— lightened up with glass block. Conrad residence, CA

Private to the street. Open to the view. NC

A study in the round.

A real library—
for booklovers.

"We designed the basic layout of our house on a

placemat in a restaurant one night, and we stayed

very close to that original concept." Debbie and Ken Wilson, NC

A window wall captures the view in the Smith residence. ON

Autumn foliage sets
off the Radwan
residence. IL

An indoor pool in the
Fritz residence. NC

small treasures

Small is beautiful when you build a Lindal original. Even our smallest

homes have a big impact. The secret is making the most of every square

foot—with open, airy post and beam construction and floorplans that

welcome a lot of living in a modest amount of space. Some Lindal owners build their small treasures for leisurely, low-maintenance getaways.

Many more live in these gems year-round—living proof that scaling

down doesn't have to mean settling for less.

The hallmarks of this series are its prow front and vaulted ceiling with open beams. Contempo Prows have small, economical floorplans, ranging

Contempo Prow

from a compact 1,173 square feet to a more spacious 1,889 square feet. Three of the four plans in this series come with a topknot. Of course, you can add a wing whenever you wish; for inspiration, see the Contempo Prow Star series on pages 68–77.

This solid cedar beauty looks out on a frozen lake not far from Anchorage. AK

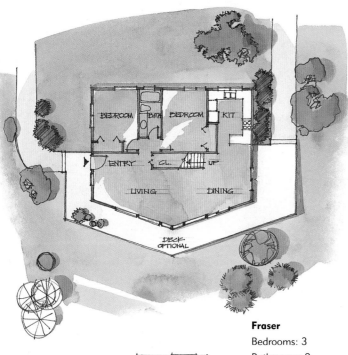

Fraser
Bedrooms: 3
Bathrooms: 2
Total Area: 1331 sq. ft.
Size: 37' x 32'

See plans at larger scale on pages 169–170.

The all-glass front of this Contempo Prow gives its Maui owners a panoramic view of Lanai and Kahoolawe. HI

Rattan furniture is perfectly suited to the casual decor of this Hawaiian home. HI

The owners of this Puget Sound vacation getaway chose solid cedar specifications. Custom residence, WA

Our Chalet series features a steeply pitched roof that reaches for the sky, and a vertical window wall that brings in the great outdoors. These homes range in size from 1,174 to 1,596 square feet. Note that three of

Chalet

the four plans have a dormer on the second floor, which substantially increases usable floor space. You can add one wherever you wish. Chalet plans with wings are shown in the Chalet Star series on pages 80–83.

Open rail stairs lead to a charming loft. CA

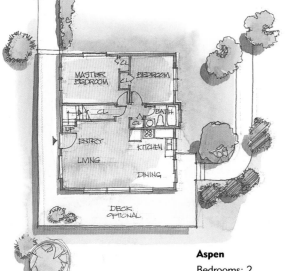

Aspen
Bedrooms: 2
Bathrooms: 1
Total Area: 1189 sq. ft.
Size: 28' x 30'

See plans at larger scale on pages 171–172.

"Once experiencing a Lindal home, nothing else could ever compare." David and Cathy Osterman, TN

The interior drama of a stone fireplace is carried through to the exterior wall, where it is a natural complement to Western red cedar. TN

Adding a dormer to the Aspen converted an open loft into a spacious master bedroom retreat. Spittlehouse residence, ON

Prows have the steeply pitched roofs characteristic of Chalets and a prow

front of glass—like the Contempo Prows, but higher. This series offers a

wide range of sizes, from a modest 768 square feet to a generous 2,489 Prow

square feet. Most plans come with a dormer, and you can always add one. If it makes sense to think small

now, it's good to know you can easily add a wing later; for ideas, see the

Prow Star series on pages 84–91.

For convenience in placing your furniture, sunrooms can be ordered on a basewall, with glass above.

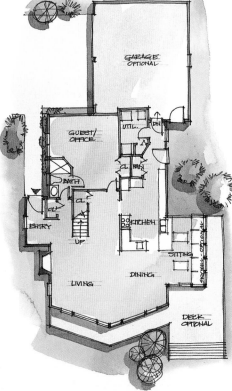

"The Prow design has given us the openness we were looking for. Also, the cedar-lined

ceiling was a last-minute decision that touched off the entire home." Rich and Helen Gibbons, NY

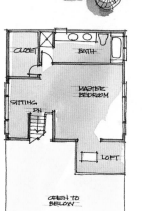

Haliburton
Bedrooms: 2
Bathrooms: 1 Full + 1 Three-quarter
Total Area: 2043 sq. ft.
Size: 37' x 47'

See plans at larger scale
on pages 173–177.

The Gibbons loft bedroom provides an inviting sanctuary for dreaming and stargazing.

Their sleek, modern kitchen is warmed up with wood touches.

"Make your dream home a reality; build a Lindal. We did!"

Prow Variations

The Russell master bedroom looks out on the golf course—and down into the living area. CA

A pool table helps put the scale of the Russell home in perspective. CA

The Moeller residence has a breathtaking view of the Pacific—and tame deer at dawn and dusk. CA

This is what dormers on the second floor can do: Create a real master bedroom retreat. CA

"Our home is three and a half years old, and we still get compliments on the fresh cedar fragrance."
John Moeller, CA

> *"A fine product, personalized service, and the best home value in the country."* Donald and Linda Russell, CA

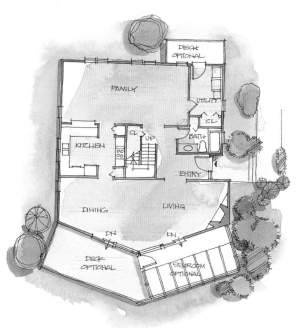

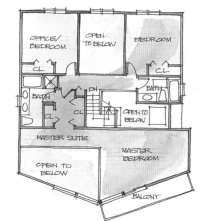

Shenandoah
Bedrooms: 3
Bathrooms: 3
Total Area: 2489 sq. ft.
Size: 39' x 42'

See plans at larger scale on pages 173–177.

The Shenandoah stretches the meaning of "small treasure," and the Russells love every square foot of their High Sierras getaway. CA

This solid cedar Prow at Tahoe is large enough to welcome a houseful of skiers. CA

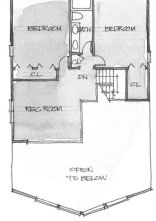

Capistrano
Bedrooms: 3
Bathrooms: 2 Full + 1 Half
Total Area: 2305 sq. ft.
Size: 32' x 48'

See plans at larger scale on pages 173–177.

Cedar's fine grain takes a wide range of stains and paints beautifully.

With a fire in the stone fireplace this custom prow in Arizona is a special place to be.

The pitched roof of this prow seems to reach the stars.

"It's a jewel nestled in the pines." Terry Ford, AZ

The loft above makes this dining room cozy and inviting.

Upstairs there's a million-dollar view from the loft.

Summit

The Summit's distinctive roof rises from gently sloping sides to a soaring chalet roof at the pinnacle. Inside, the sense of drama is heightened by a panoramic prow front, with its floor-to-ceiling glass rising to a lofty peak. All plans have full master bedroom suites with dormers on the second floor. However, it's easy to relocate the suite to the main level, if you wish. Summits with wings are shown in the Summit Star series on pages 96–97.

The natural beauty of the cedar timbers and wood ceilings is enriched by the stone fireplace.

"In the winter, we feel so snug with the fireplace going and the cold and rain outside." Homeowner, WA

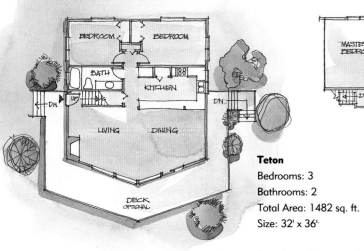
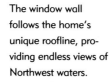

Teton
Bedrooms: 3
Bathrooms: 2
Total Area: 1482 sq. ft.
Size: 32' x 36'

See plans at larger scale on pages 179–181.

The window wall follows the home's unique roofline, providing endless views of Northwest waters.

The distinctive roofline is the signature of our Summit series. WA

With a skylight and
cedar overhead and
lots of windows, the
Villeneuve kitchen
is a pleasure to
work in. CA

Shed dormers signifi-
cantly increase usable
living space upstairs. MI

"Our home stays very warm even in the worst of Colorado winter storms

Accents of Western
red cedar showcase
its infinite variety of
color and pattern. CA

"We decided Lindal's
striking designs and
natural wood exteriors
would blend beauti-
fully with our wooded
seacoast site."
Donald Villeneuve, CA

Cedar's radiant colors range from a warm gold to a burnished red.

at the 9,500-foot elevation." David Jenkins, CO

Castle Rock Mountain, near Purgatory Ski Resort, provides a magnificent backdrop for the Jenkins' vacation home. CO

Why not add swinging patio doors to a deck outside? WA

Simple but striking, our View homes bring together the best of Lindal in a small package: the beauty of Western red cedar, the drama of open-beamed ceilings, and a window wall to the outdoors. You can build View *a View home on a slab or a full or daylight basement. In fact, because so many View homes are built on hillside sites, one plan is drawn with a daylight basement. In the right location, that can double your view.*

The living room window wall frames a sweeping view of forest and sea on the Sunshine coast. BC

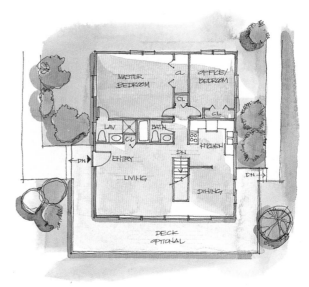

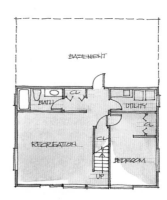

Waikiki II
Bedrooms: 3
Bathrooms: 2 Full + 1 Three-quarter
Total Area: 1744 sq. ft.
Size: 32' x 37'

See plans at larger scale on pages 182–184.

"We are glad we chose Lindal. After a hectic, busy day it is so nice to be welcomed by a relaxed, cordial atmosphere. I would be pleased to recommend Lindal homes to anyone." Sharon Wood, BC

Every square foot of the Wood residence takes full advantage of its water view— including the daylight basement. BC

Panorama

Take full advantage of a wide view site with a Panorama plan. The entire front wall of glass is designed to take in the scenic grandeur all around you. Inside, the ceiling is vaulted with open beams. The roomy, U-shaped Monaco plan comes with bonus space in the loft. Consider an optional topknot to raise the height of the low loft and create enough space for a media room, a library—a private retreat.

A light, airy sunroom creates a charming sitting area just off the Vasilik master bedroom—with room for an exercise bicycle and easel too. NC

OPTIONAL TOP KNOT

MEDIA ROOM

Monaco II
Bedrooms: 3
Bathrooms: 1 Full + 1 Three-quarter
Total Area: 1564 sq. ft.
Size: 43' x 37'

See plans at larger scale on page 185.

"Three thousand miles from your factory to our site, down a narrow three-mile dirt road, delivered on time, within the price quotes." Christopher and Shirley Sherrill, NH

The owners added astral glass front and back—creating a see-through view with an appealing sense of openness. ON

A wall of glass gives this Smith Mountain Lake home a striking indoor-outdoor beauty. Riddick model home, VA

Pole homes are the ideal solution to challenging hillside sites, beaches where flooding may occur, Texas ranchlands—anywhere you want to raise Pole *your home above the ground. Aesthetically, these homes have a special character, a poetic stance that sets them apart. Their wraparound decks, sheltered by deep overhanging roofs, are perfectly suited to sites from the Gulf States to tropical zones worldwide.*

"My home is airtight to drafts and insulated so you are warm in winter and cool in summer without it costing an arm and a leg in electricity." Nancy Crowe, TX

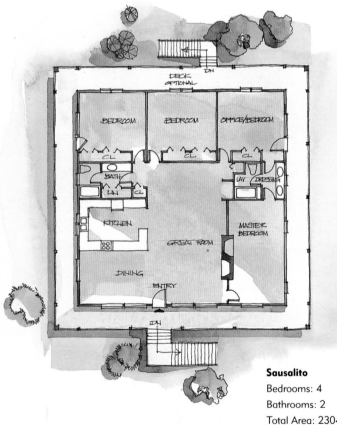

Sausalito
Bedrooms: 4
Bathrooms: 2
Total Area: 2304 sq. ft.
Size: 48' x 48'

See plans at larger scale on page 187.

"When I see my home in the distance, my heartbeat increases and my foot gets heavy on the pedal." Nancy Crowe, TX

Gambrel

Our Gambrel series is named for its traditional roof style, which wraps down to form much of the walls of the second floor. In addition to giving these homes a distinctive style, this roof makes Gambrels extremely energy efficient. And two-story construction on a small footprint makes them exceptionally cost-effective, too. Variations are shown in the Heritage and Colonial series on pages 124–125.

Your local Lindal consultant will help you modify your plan to incorporate the kitchen you've always wanted. ON

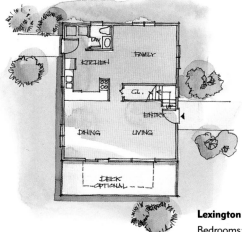
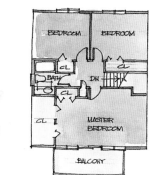

Lexington
Bedrooms: 3
Bathrooms: 1 Full + 1 Half
Total Area: 1615 sq. ft.
Size: 27' x 31'

See plans at larger scale on page 186.

The Canzanellis started with the Lexington and modified it by adding a wing for even more space. MA

contemporary

Allow us to introduce our most dramatic statements: Lindal's Contemporary homes are the height of bold design. Imagine soaring rooflines. Panoramic prow fronts. Walls of windows. Cathedral ceilings that create a sweeping interior spaciousness. Yet their stunning appearance is just the beginning of their beauty; Lindal Contemporaries are intelligent designs for living. Their expansive sense of freedom is much more than a look; it's a way of life that contemporary homeowners love to come home to.

Sliding glass doors from the nine-bay sunroom, living room and master bedroom provide easy access to an expansive wraparound deck overlooking the water.

Contempo Prow Star

If you like the architectural style of a prow and a vaulted ceiling, consider our Contempo Prow Stars. These spacious contemporaries range in size from 1,514 to 3,480 square feet, with wings on one or both sides of the prow. This series has the lowest-pitched roofline of all Lindal prows —ideal when building regulations dictate roof heights. Let's begin with the Butler home in Quebec.

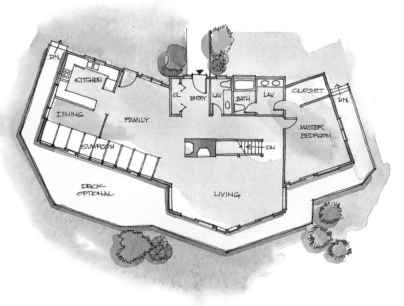

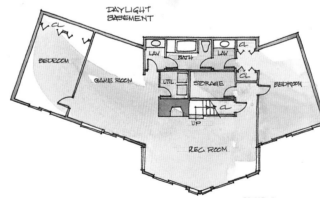

CliffSide
Bedrooms: 3
Bathrooms: 2 Full + 1 Half
Total Area: 3480 sq. ft.
Size: 73' x 41'

See plans at larger scale on pages 188–194.

Easygoing luxury: Sumptuous furnishings and a view-oriented window wall make this living room a most inviting place to linger a while.

Variations

The flexibility of Lindal design gives you endless possibilities for personal

variations. Each of the homes you see here is a living reminder that our

design library is only the beginning of the possibilities.

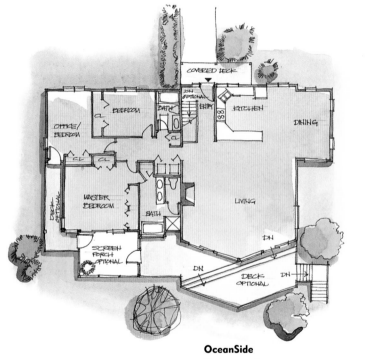

OceanSide
Bedrooms: 3
Bathrooms: 2
Total Area: 2062 sq. ft.
Size: 66' x 40'

See plan at larger scale
on page 191.

"We are most pleased with our Lindal home. The quality of the Lindal components is A-1;

The Faulstich home
is private and pro-
tective on the street
side. Floorplan shown
at left. NC

"The large windows
and glass doors provide
us with a view from
every room." Jerry and
Helen Faulstich, NC

A sunroom floods the kitchen of the Porter residence with natural light and provides a panoramic view of Lake Superior. ON

Brick and cedar create a handsome exterior on the Porter custom residence. ON

The Porter window wall transforms their dining room into an open, airy space. ON

they made the construction of our home smoother than we anticipated." John and Martha Worley, MA

An aerial view of the Worley home and complementary boathouse on a lake southeast of Boston. MA

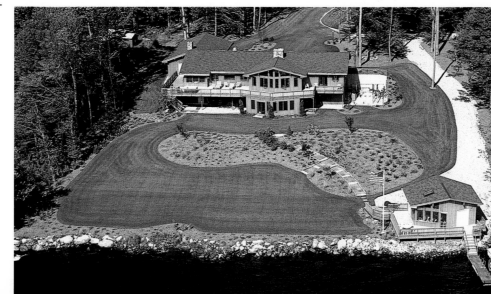

Another view of the exterior of the Mendes cedar clapboard home is shown on the inside front cover of this book. CA

Situated above a spacious walkout basement, this prow cuts a dramatic profile against a backdrop of snow-capped mountains. AK

"The design flexibility made our ideas come to life. We had the final say." Mr. and Mrs. Mendes, CA

An exterior view of the Case residence is shown on the inside back cover of this book. VA

"Anytime guests visit or people stop by, they marvel at our home, its construction and the view." Phil and Margot Case, VA

Deer Parks

The gently-peaked Contempo Prow Star style was the inspiration for Deer Parks, a Lindal original built by Sherman Parks and Georgia Jenkins Parks. The story of their dream home's design and construction is chronicled on pages 6, 9, 16, 76-77, and 263.

The Parks built their solid cedar Lindal original in their own private paradise, on 15 acres of forest in Washougal, Washington.

The solid cedar richness of the Parks kitchen is accented by crisp white custom cabinetry and the infusion of natural light from the windows and skylight.

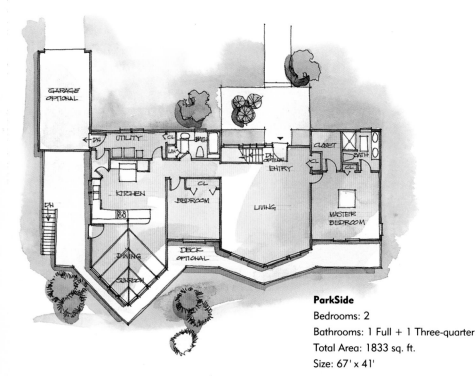

ParkSide
Bedrooms: 2
Bathrooms: 1 Full + 1 Three-quarter
Total Area: 1833 sq. ft.
Size: 67' x 41'

See plan at larger scale
on page 190.

Winter, spring, summer and fall, the stunning sun/dining room is the Parks' favorite room in the house.

"We would recommend Lindal to anyone who does not want to settle for an off-the-rack, stick-built home when it is possible to have an original home for the same price." Georgia Parks, WA

This journal is lovingly dedicated to Georgia's parents, Laverne and Ferrol Jenkins, whose generous wisdom and support were invaluable.

MAY

My cousin cheerfully volunteered his professional expertise and engineered all the concrete work. (The subcontractors said they don't even build high-rises as well as our foundation!) Sherman water-proofed the foundation walls, installed a French drain below the footing to prevent water buildup, and applied closed-cell foam insulation to the outer wall. Our consultant, Ole, has been great about helping us "newcomers" find the best subcontractors.

Georgia

JUNE

Our very first wall went up early this month. By the end of the month, the cedar siding was on most of our home, including the guest bedroom and the art studio. When Georgia first saw the cedar in all its radiant glory, she spent a lot of time just staring at it and exclaiming, "It's gorgeous!" Ole has saved the day more than once by helping me make design changes that meet Georgia's desires for dramatic design and my concerns for functionality.

Sherman

JULY–AUGUST

While Sherman was away on a 13-day trip to Japan, the second story began to take shape. The weather was perfect and progress was dramatic. The beams are so impressive! Some good friends from Colorado Springs visited us—and were promptly drafted to help install our well pump. In one day, we saved $1,000 and discovered we had nothing to fear but fear itself. The water tastes great and comes out of the well at 65 gallons a minute. Life is good.

Georgia

Continued from page 16

AUGUST–SEPTEMBER

Sherman installed all our electrical to
exceed minimum code—to the point that
the building inspector said we were
wasting money. Yet we still saved about
$15,000. The fireproof metal roof was
a challenge; because of my design, no
company wanted any part of it! Family
and friends pitched in and worked with
Sherman 13 hours a day to get it on
before the rain began. We won. Again,
we had nothing to fear but fear itself.

Life is still good.

Georgia

OCTOBER 21–22

Our family is the greatest painting crew!
Free labor—plus they bring the food!
They came from all over Oregon, bringing
sleeping bags and campers and staying
overnight for a two-day painting marathon.
They came armed with brushes, spray guns,
buckets, sandpaper, paint thinner—and the
food. We painted, applied oil inside and
water sealer outside, and completely covered
the interior and exterior in one weekend.

Sherman

NOVEMBER–DECEMBER

Surprise—custom cabinets are cheaper than
store-bought! Solid wood, too—and
the price included a pro to install them.
Happy day; the house begins to look
finished. Let it rain. Let it snow.
We even have heat and air conditioning,
running water and lights. Sherman and son
are now taking the time to sit on the deck,
smoke a cigar, have a beer, and watch the
beautiful sunsets. Ole and company actually
worked Christmas week and weekend to
meet the deadline for our occupancy permit!

Georgia

Conclusion on page 263

The second-story loft houses a light, airy library with a view of the backyard—and plenty of room for books and bibliophiles.

Some Lindal homeowners have taken our Contempo Prow Stars to new heights of spaciousness and grandeur—by adding a second story. For Tom and Sue Button, a second story was an ideal way to get the extra

Building Up

room, the "treetop" feeling and the lofty views they wanted for their solid cedar Lindal. They added an extra bedroom and bathroom and located the second-floor master bedroom suite to take in the best views of their 18-acre woodland site.

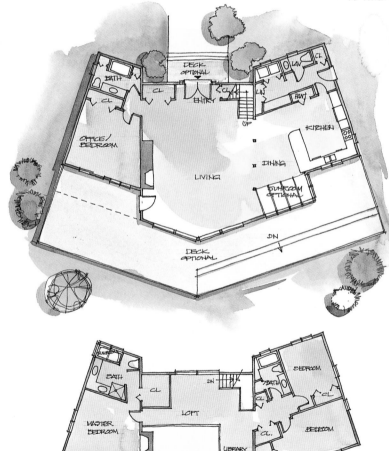

"The flexibility of Lindal's system is just incredible. We have a Justus (solid cedar home), but were able to incorporate several features from your frame homes." Tom and Sue Button, WA

CountrySide
Bedrooms: 4
Bathrooms: 3 Full + 1 Half
Total Area: 3183 sq. ft.
Size: 69' x 44'

See plans at larger scale on pages 195–196.

With its site-sensitive design and solid cedar beauty, the Button residence is very much at home on its 18 forested acres in Washington. Its two-story wall of windows looks out to a creek that flows into the nearby Columbia River.

A bright, airy sun-room is located just off the office/guest room in the Schutz/Roggenbuck home. ON

With their cathedral ceilings and window walls that take in the world around them, these Lindal Contemporaries are perennial favorites. Chalet

Chalet Star

Stars have wings, which encourages design-wise zoning. Spacious master bedroom suites with dormers are

located on the second floor for an appealing sense of privacy. These homes

range in size from 1,460 to 2,188 square feet.

The upstairs master bedroom is open to a glamorous whirlpool tub.

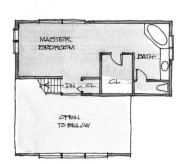

FairHill
Bedrooms: 3
Bathrooms: 2
Total Area: 2188 sq. ft.
Size: 56' x 30'

See plans at larger scale on pages 197–200.

Notice the topknot over the ridge on the wing? That's the master bath. Also note that the cedar siding is stained driftwood gray.

Western red cedar grows in its native habitat of the Pacific Northwest.

Two Chalet Stars—
two looks: living
room to loft and living
room to window wall.
NJ & ON

A massive fireplace
built of local stone is
the centerpiece of this
Lindal in Ohio.

The Freitags are
serious cedar lovers,
as their living room
proves. WI

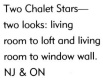

"Lindal and our consultant worked with our local

architect and executed the design flawlessly." Rick and Bobbi Freitag, WI

"Lindal was able to
engineer a four-gable
roof with vaulted
ceiling and lots of
windows which let
daylight in from all
directions." WI

Native Americans used Western red cedar to build post and beam dwellings of massive size and strength.

Prow Star

Prow Stars are our best sellers—and with their dramatically high roofs, glass-fronted prows and two-story views, it's easy to see why. These roomy designs include lower-pitched wings on one or both sides. You'll find a wide range of plans for these homes in our design library, varying in size from 1,387 to over 3,000 square feet.

Notice the topknot over the lower-pitched wing on the right? That's the master bath.

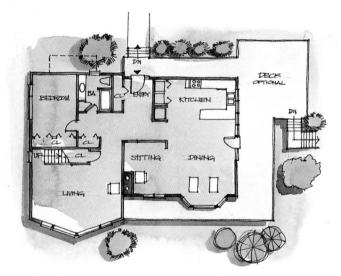

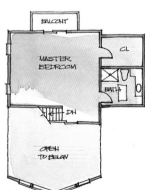

LakeVista
Bedrooms: 2
Bathrooms: 1 Full + 1 Three-quarter
Total Area: 2017 sq. ft.
Size: 47' x 37'

See plans at larger scale on pages 201–211.

"We get rave reviews from everyone who comes our way— whether it's family, friends or the UPS delivery man!" Gail Denemark and Gary Ksander, NJ

A skylight over the four-poster and bleached timbers create an airy look.

The high ceiling and exposed beams frame the view perfectly.

In the bright dining area, country decor works hand in hand with the solid cedar timbers and hardwood flooring.

"What we like best is the openness.

We love the cedar—it is so

warm and rich looking." Duane and Jeannette Moorman, TN

The massive fireplace, steep-pitched cedar ceiling, spiral staircase and open loft add a lodge-like grandeur. TN

The floorplan provides an uninterrupted flow between kitchen, dining and living room. TN

Reaching up to capture the light, cedar trees grow tall and straight, with trunks free of branches for much of their height.

The O'Briens lovingly
designed the kitchen
to celebrate "what-
ever's cooking." CA

Another exterior
view of the O'Brien
cedar clapboard
home is shown on
page 162. CA

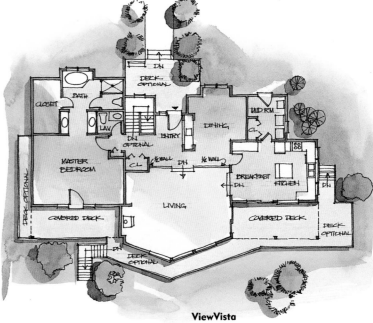

ViewVista

Bedrooms: 1
Bathrooms: 1 Full + 1 Half
Total Area: 1920 sq. ft.
Size: 67' x 43'

See plan at larger scale
on page 207.

87

Gluck Residence, ON

In the Fritz residence, a high cathedral ceiling glows with the radiance of Western red cedar. NC

Antique furnishings add elegance and a traditional flair to the Fritz residence. NC

The master bath is a luxurious retreat, complete with Italian marble. NC

The Rosses use their loft for games and a library. WA

Paradise found: "Our home and location are the result of a thirteen-year search for this setting on the east fork of the Lewis River." Mr. and Mrs. Ross, WA

This Prow Star reflects the beauty of its location on Big Rideau Lake, south of Ottawa. ON

Here we've built on inspiration. These designs begin with the same high-profile prow front as our Prow Star series—and take the rest of the

Prows with 2 Story Wings

home to new heights with a two-story wing that adds economical floor space. The roofline of the single-story garage is also extended to create the effect of a covered veranda across the front facade of the two-story wing.

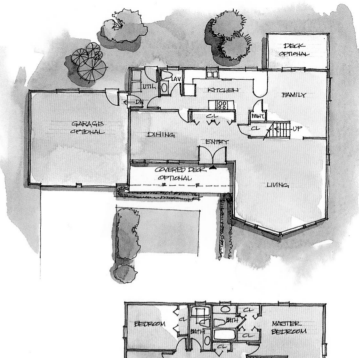

WoodLawn
Bedrooms: 3
Bathrooms: 2 Full + 1 Half
Total Area: 2042 sq. ft.
Size: 46' x 38'

See plans at larger scale
on pages 212–213.

Diagonally placed
cedar directs all eyes to
the park-like view. NJ

A back and side view
of the Boursy home
shows how well it
follows the lay of
the land. CT

The Boursys started
with the WoodLawn,
but extended living
space into the garage;
then built the garage
underneath. Boursy
residence, CT

The lustrous colors and velvety finish of Western red cedar make it a daily delight to live with.

Prows with 1 & 2 Story Wings

These Prow Stars feature both a single-story and a two-story wing—

increasing living space even more and adding architectural interest. The

WoodLand and WoodHaven plans are found on pages 214 and 215.

Creative homeowners in Massachusetts inspired the Wood-Haven plan, shown above, below and to the right.

Anything goes! Add a tower if you like (and if your code permits). MA

The spiral staircase in the master bedroom leads to the observatory. MA

Variation on a theme: The DeBerry residence, a WoodLand. MA

"We are very happy with the service we received during the

ordering, building and finishing of our home." Larry and Laura DeBerry, MA

Elegant furnishings, fabulous view; it's not every home that has a view of hot air balloons from its living room windows. MA

A bird's-eye view of the Millers' kitchen, and two storage ideas. VA

If you like the distinctive roofline and prow front of our Summit model

but need more space, you're not alone. A number of Lindal homeowners

have seen a need—and the appeal—of adding wings to Summit models.

Summit Star

We're proud to dedicate our new Summit Star series to them. You can opt for a one-story wing on one

or both sides. Most families centralize their shared living space in the

"Summit" and locate their quiet, private spaces in a wing.

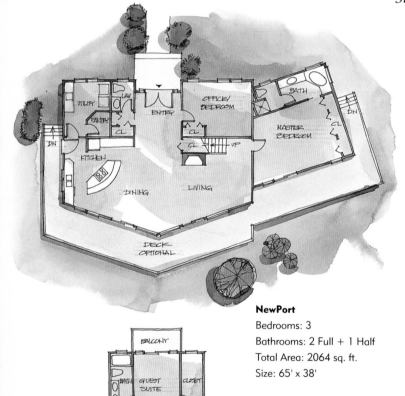

NewPort
Bedrooms: 3
Bathrooms: 2 Full + 1 Half
Total Area: 2064 sq. ft.
Size: 65' x 38'

See plans at larger scale on pages 216–217.

The Kelley home in Connecticut inspired our NewPort.

White-washed custom cabinets are a pristine counterpoint to the warmth of this kitchen's hardwood floors and cedar ceiling. Miller residence, VA

"We chose Lindal Cedar Homes because we wanted an open floorplan. The kitchen,

dining room and living room are combined into one large great room." Dotty Kelley, CT

classic

What makes a Classic? At Lindal, it's a sense of casual elegance and livability that never goes out of style—the inspiration for a diverse collection of some of the most appealing homes in residential design today.

Many feature multiple levels, long rooflines and interiors that welcome the use of vaulted ceilings, window walls and sunrooms. You'll find there's a Classic design for just about any site—from spacious suburban properties to narrow city lots. You'll also find that their timeless architectural character makes them at home in fine residential neighborhoods anywhere.

Design your bath exactly the way you want it: these home-owners did. OR

Lindal Ranches are planned for harmonious living. In this popular series, two wings join at right angles to form an "L"—with the bedrooms in one wing, living areas in the other. All rooms have vaulted ceilings and open beams for a spacious, airy appeal. Since many Ranches are built

Ranch

on sloped lots, the plans provide for stairs that make it easy to add a walkout daylight basement below. That doubles your floor space (but not your costs). The smaller plan is 1,500 square feet; the larger is 2,700 square feet.

Silverado
Bedrooms: 3
Bathrooms: 2
Total Area: 2700 sq. ft.
Size: 66' x 56'

See plans at larger scale on pages 218–219.

What architecture could be more at home in nature's beauty than a Lindal? CA

At dusk, the cedar has a mystical glow in this home in the Santa Ynez ranch country. CA

chapter **5**

CLASSIC

If zoning your family's activities into separate areas is important, take a look at the way these split-levels locate them on different floors. Both of

Split Level

the floorplans achieve this, each in its own way. Common strengths: a high ceiling that enhances the spacious feeling of the living and family areas on the main level—while the master suite and family room take advantage of the high peaked ceilings and open beams on the top level.

The owners of this stunning split-level home opted for a screened porch instead of a sunroom and added a garage. VA

Tuscany
Bedrooms: 3 + Bonus Room
Bathrooms: 2
Total Area: 1616 sq. ft.
Size: 37' x 31'

See plans at larger scale
on pages 220–221.

"My home design is my own, using one of your plans for a guide."
Mike Corbeil, ON

"I am amazed at how cozy and warm the house is, even on the blustery winter nights. Despite the large glass area, the house is very comfortable summer or winter. It's easy to heat, and easy to cool."
Homeowners, VA

The new College series offers yet another interpretation of multi-level

design. Changing rooflines add visual interest. Expansive glass areas let

in the view and bathe the home with more light. Both models share an easy elegance that feels timeless and

true. The Harvard is 2,393 square feet; the Princeton is just over

3,000 square feet.

College

Laurie and Lloyd
Gilbert say their
home gives them "the
pleasure of living in a
constantly changing
landscape." ON

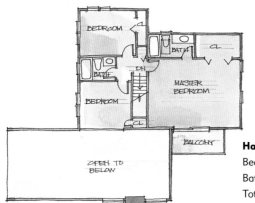

The Gilberts zoned
their sitting room/
study to a lower level.

Harvard
Bedrooms: 3 + Office
Bathrooms: 2 Full + 1 Half
Total Area: 2393 sq. ft.
Size: 53' x 43'

See plans at larger scale
on pages 222–223.

Native Americans used Western red cedar in everything from houses and canoes to baskets and ceremonial objects.

"One of the most
enjoyable features of
our home is the very
effective use of large
expanses of glass."

Pavilion

These Lindal homes bring the romance of pavilion architecture to every-day life. The focal point is a large, multi-sided pavilion, dedicated to family living areas and beautifully integrated into the rest of the home. In the smaller Starlight, the master bedroom is on the main floor. In the larger Stargazer, it's on the second floor.

"We wanted lots of glass, to take advantage of the water view." Pam Jackson and Pat Archer, ON

"We wanted wood, and the name Lindal came up as we both associated it with quality."

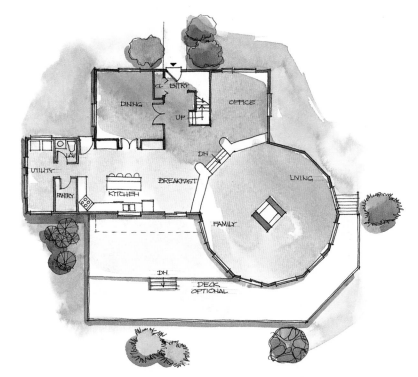

Stargazer
Bedrooms: 4 + Office
Bathrooms: 2 Full + 1 Half
Total Area: 3589 sq. ft.
Size: 73' x 49'

See plans at larger scale on pages 224–225.

The ceiling structure in the living room of the Pavilion is a thing of beauty in itself.

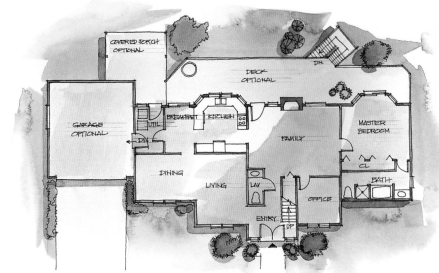

Executive

Welcome to the pride of the neighborhood. Our Executive homes have a distinctive elegance that makes them good neighbors and wonderful places to live. The street appeal of their timeless design includes stepped-down roofs, clerestory windows and the strong symmetry of the front entry. Inside, the central foyer opens up to an airy, two-story cathedral ceiling. A vaulted ceiling adds an even greater sense of space to the family room.

Georgetown
Bedrooms: 3 + Office + Bonus Room
Bathrooms: 1 Full + 1 Three-quarter + 1 Half
Total Area: 2226 sq. ft.
Size: 64' x 32'

See plans at larger scale
on pages 226–227.

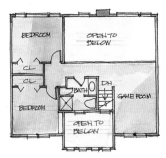

This home, built near Cincinnati in the 1970s, was an early inspiration for our Executive series. OH

The DiGiovanni dining room is enriched with antique furnishings, Oriental rugs—and the lustrous beauty of cedar. MA

"We can hardly express our pleasure in living in this lovely home." Don and Carole Forbes, VA

A gabled screen porch is one of the many ways in which the Forbes personalized their home. VA

The restrictions of a narrow urban lot seem to disappear when you take

inspiration from our City series. Designed especially for narrow lots and

City

city views, these homes present a private facade to the street, while the

interior opens up to a two-story sunroom in the living room. All in all, their rare sense of seclusion is an

elegant outlook on city living. The compact Hillsborough is 1,726 square

feet; the more spacious Westchester is nearly double the size.

In this rendition, there's a sunroom off the kitchen and mini-blinds control light and privacy. ON

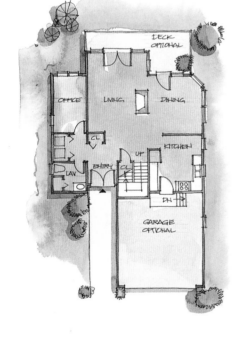

"Our consultant has been outstanding always." Homeowner, MA

A garage buffers the home from street noise, while clerestory windows admit light but protect privacy. MA

Hillsborough
Bedrooms: 3 + Office
Bathrooms: 2 Full + 1 Half
Total Area: 1726 sq. ft.
Size: 35' x 33'

See plans at larger scale
on pages 228–229.

Desiring a sophisti-cated decor, the owners of this elegant urban home painted all interior wood detailing for a seam-less look. Custom residence, MA

The idyllic view is captured by sunwalls topping a bank of sliding glass doors. Brigida residence, MA

Signature

At face value, our Signature homes may appear to have been designed for streetfront elegance alone. But take a look at the back of the house. On the second floor, sunwalls top a bank of sliding glass doors—making the most of a favorite view. The master suite is located on the second floor of the smaller plan, and on the main floor of the larger one.

Plaid upholstery and a braid rug add a rustic charm inside. SC

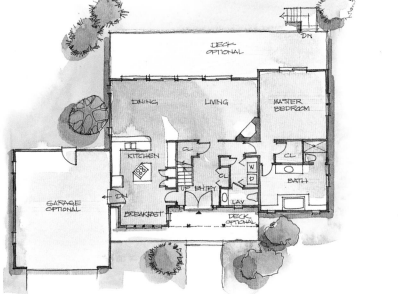

Hallmark

Bedrooms: 3 + Bonus Room
Bathrooms: 2 Full + 1 Half
Total Area: 2346 sq. ft.
Size: 50' x 35'

See plans at larger scale on pages 230–231.

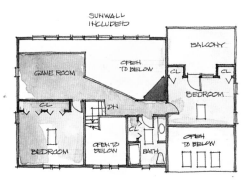

The multiple roof pitches and covered entry give the Brigida home a classic street presence. MA

"Our Lindal consultant was with us 110 percent of the way." Guy and Ann Brigida, MA

What "welcome home" could be more inviting than a two-story sun-room? It's the grand entrance of our Designer homes—with plenty of room to provide a cherished living space and give an airy openness to the Designer *entire home. Of course, even this feature can be changed, or moved to the back or view side, as you'll see in the variations ahead. All of these modern classics feature an appealing mix of exterior rooflines; inside, cathedral ceilings provide a spacious feeling to the living, dining and upstairs areas.*

"The post and beam construction makes an open, free-flowing floor plan. It's light and airy at all times."

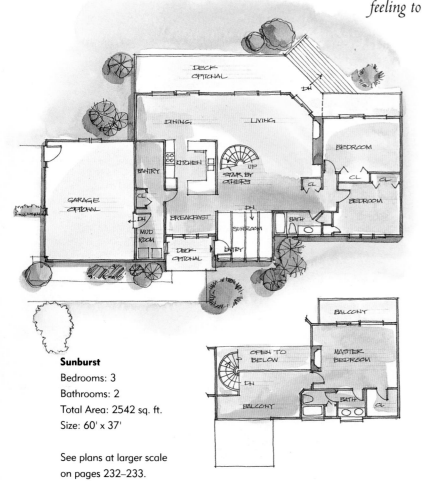

Sunburst
Bedrooms: 3
Bathrooms: 2
Total Area: 2542 sq. ft.
Size: 60' x 37'

See plans at larger scale on pages 232–233.

With a screened porch, eating out of doors is irresistible and comfortable.

From the lake the large scale of the Feroe home can best be appreciated.

"Thank-you notes from our friends are as ecstatic as we are:

'Gorgeous, splendid, so beautiful, an elegant residence, lovely ambience.'" Dick and Jo Feroe, VA

Natural stone complements the driftwood-gray stain.

One glimpse of their glorious mountain view explains why the Rutherfords switched their sunroom from the entry to the view side. ID

Built on a daylight basement to accommodate its sloping site, the Morden-Boughton home rises to three stories. ON

The daylight basement facade is faced with local stone, a pleasing complement to the natural cedar above. ON

The massive fireplace and hunting trophies are shown off against a backdrop of white drywall and rich cedar detailing. ON

"Our consultant was extremely helpful in overseeing the construction (in Sun Valley), since we were living in Virginia." Bill and Florence Rutherford, ID

"We love the openness our home offers to take advantage of the exquisite views of the river and the mountains." Bill Rutherford, ID

This is the entry or street side of the Rutherford home. An exterior of the view side is shown on page 244. ID

Solid cedar timber construction was the clear preference of the Moreno family for their vacation home in Tennessee, shown above and to the right.

At dusk there's a special magic to the Foster home, which has inspired countless others to design a personalized rendition. WA

The Hynnes sunroom opens to a large, well-used deck for outdoor living. ON

The Hynnes incorporated a spacious sunroom into their kitchen, making it the favorite gathering spot in their home. ON

"We have great pride of ownership in our home, made of the best natural materials—cedar and stone." Bruce and Bev Hynnes, ON

traditional

Create a landmark in your own time with a Lindal Traditional, and

you'll have a home worth handing down for generations to come. These

are homes with a heritage. Inspired by the rich history of North American

residential architecture, they combine the style, quality materials and craftsmanship of yesterday with all the comforts and conveniences of today.

There aren't many opportunities in life to enjoy the finest of the past and

the present. But a Lindal Traditional is one of them.

"The use of cedar on the inside is quite spectacular, contrasted with the off-white drywall."

A front view of this home's exterior is shown on page 120.

The timeless charm of our traditional Cape design is true to its roots —with a central entry, covered porch and steep gabled roof with gable dormers. Inside, we've taken the liberty to lighten things up by design, creating a modern living space that's spacious and bright. Clapboard siding and corner boards are tradition- ally part of the Cape style. But you can opt for Classic siding, Round Log or Solid Cedar. As always, the choice is yours.

Cape

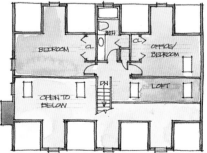

Cape Breton
Bedrooms: 3
Bathrooms: 2 Full + 1 Three-quarter
Total Area: 2533 sq. ft.
Size: 62' x 34'

See plans at larger scale
on page 234.

"It's a home that never will be boring or mundane."

"The quality of materials supplied by your company is top grade." Homeowner, WA

Feel free to add an island or a garden window to make our kitchen yours alone. ON

Tudor

True to their fabled ancestors, our Tudors have high-pitched gabled roofs, functional shed dormers, and covered porches. In the Cotswold plan, the high-pitched garage joins the house at right angles to become an integral part of the overall design. This home has street presence.

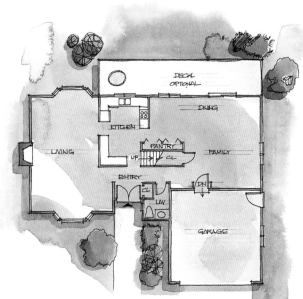

Cotswold
Bedrooms: 4 + Office
Bathrooms: 2 Full + 1 Half
Total Area: 3075 sq. ft.
Size: 54' x 43'

See plans at larger scale on page 235.

Shed dormers add light—and charm—to the upstairs bedroom and study. WA

Beloved family heir-
looms—silver, crystal,
porcelain and antique
furniture—grace the
dining room. NY

No other roof design provides the protective, sheltering style of a gambrel.

But its snug coziness is more than a look: since the roof wraps down to

form most of the upper floor's outside walls, it creates a high R-value ## Heritage

that makes Heritage homes especially energy efficient. Both plans have two full floors—a cost-effective way

to build in lots of living space. One-story wings add even more space and

graceful lines to the design.

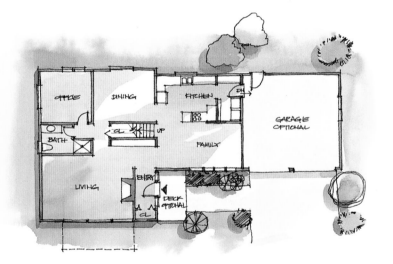

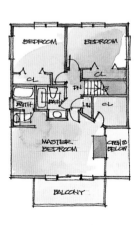

Yorktown
Bedrooms: 3 + Office
Bathrooms: 2 Full + 1 Three-quarter
Total Area: 2151 sq. ft.
Size: 47' x 34'

See plans at larger scale
on pages 236–237.

Surrounded by a
blaze of fall color, this
Gambrel is at home
in the historic Hudson
Valley. NY

"We love this home. Every part of it! We recommend your company to anyone who wants to live elegantly and expects practicality." Mr. and Mrs. DeVajay, NY

Before remodel: 1000
square feet. NY

Colonial

In this version of a Gambrel, the second floor has been cropped to a loft—

creating a cathedral ceiling and two-story windows. Of course, anything

is possible, as the home at right shows so well. Its owners added a second

intersecting Colonial to the original core Gambrel, tripling living area.

After remodel: 3300
square feet.

"If you wish to use our home as an example of how

easy it is to add to an existing Lindal home, you may." Homeowner, NY

Mayflower
Bedrooms: 3
Bathrooms: 2
Total Area: 1907 sq. ft.
Size: 48' x 35'

See plans at larger scale
on page 238.

A Mayflower plan
over an optional full
basement. NY

New England

The strong, sheltering lines of the gambrel roof are a dominant element of New England architecture—and of this traditional Lindal. These homes have an inviting sense of symmetry, with a front central entry flanked by bow windows on both sides and gable dormers above. A full second floor is an economical way to create more living space.

Even in the rain, a two-story sunroom is a special place to be.

A Palladian window, framed in Douglas fir, complements the elegant antique furnishings in this traditional home.

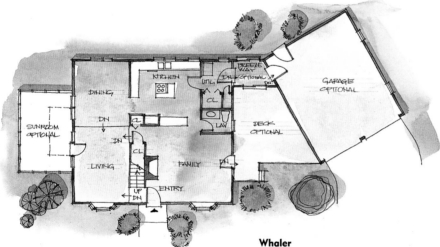

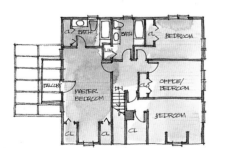

Whaler
Bedrooms: 4
Bathrooms: 2 Full + 1 Half
Total Area: 2327 sq. ft.
Size: 37' x 32'

See plans at larger scale on pages 239–240

The Whaler, pictured here, showcases a smart option for security and year-round comfort: an enclosed breezeway to the garage. Custom residence, MA

Aptly enough, the actual Native American word for Western red cedar translates as "dry underneath."

Liberty

"Liberty" is the word for the sense of freedom you get from the moment you walk into these homes. Their architectural focal point is the two-story picture window dormer, a contemporary accent that opens up the center of the massive gambrel roof and floods the interior with natural light. Cathedral ceilings rise to eighteen feet over the central living, or family, room. Upstairs, an open gallery connects the two bedroom wings.

There's a bird's-eye view of the living room from the gallery above. NC

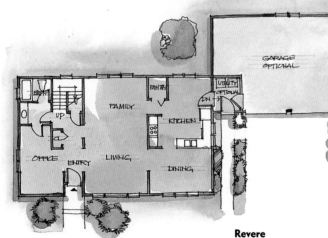

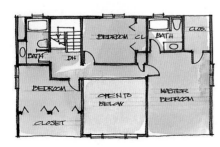

Revere
Bedrooms: 3 + Office
Bathrooms: 3
Total Area: 2172 sq. ft.
Size: 45' x 27'

See plans at larger scale on pages 241–242.

The massive gambrel roof makes Liberty homes energy misers. NY

"We have to be the most satisfied customers Lindal can possibly have, and your consultant is a friend

Farmhouse

Perhaps no architectural vernacular stirs greater love for home and land than the Farmhouse. Ours maintains the rustic romance of the original —with a few appealing refinements. We've dormered the steeply pitched roof across the front to expand useful living space upstairs. And the most popular addition of all is the covered veranda, ideal for all those times when you just want to sit and watch the world go by.

A Round Log facade is shown here, but the Farmhouse is also available in Lindal's Classic siding, Clapboard siding, or Solid Cedar timbers. MI

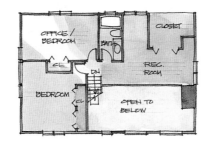

Pioneer
Bedrooms: 3
Bathrooms: 2 Full + 1 Half
Total Area: 1867 sq. ft.
Size: 40' x 27'

See plans at larger scale on page 243.

As the bedroom shows, it's easy to change windows and doors to suit yourself. ON

we will always have." Gene and Denise Fiorot, NY

home planning ideas

Your ideas. Your priorities. Your personal sense of beauty, comfort and style. That's what planning—and living in—a Lindal original is all about. Bringing your dreams and ideas into focus and putting them down on paper is one of the great pleasures of planning your home. And it's surprisingly easy to do when you get off to the right start. With that in mind, this chapter is devoted to helping you ask, and answer, all the right questions as you plan your home. For most people, this is one of the most exciting steps in building their own Lindal—exceeded only, of course, by the finished results.

A little searching of your soul and site early on will pay off throughout

the planning and building of your Lindal original. So give yourself time

The Secrets to Getting Started

to think about three key issues: your wants and needs, the nature of

your building site and your budget. Together, they'll help you shape

your dreams into a graceful, coherent design that's a joy to live with.

Take Note of Your Wants and Needs
If you haven't already started a wish list, now's the time to get the family together and put your dreams down on paper. A kitchen fit for two cooks and a gathering of guests? A sun-filled family room? A place to showcase a special collection or an heirloom? At this early stage, don't dismiss anything as impractical or extravagant; have fun and let the ideas flow.

Next, take a realistic look at your wish list and divide it into "wants" and "needs." What can't you live without?

What's icing on the cake? Three bedrooms may be a must; but is an adjoining bath for each one really necessary? Only you can decide; what's frivolous to one person may be essential to another.

Now you're ready to get into more detail. We suggest you do it by keeping a notebook or design file for each area of your home. Fill it with everything that helps you envision and express your dream: magazine articles, photos, product literature, color swatches, paint chips—and, of course, your own notes.

Get to Know Your Site
The most beautiful and functional homes are a synergy of structure and site. So take ample time to identify the views you want to capture. Walk your property at different times of day—and night. Note the ebb and flow of light, the sun's changing path and the way wind and air move across the site. Consider how changing seasons will affect it.

Develop a Site Plan
Now's the time to draw a working site plan. Sketch in the property lines, ground slope, roads, power, water and gas mains, nearby buildings and any natural features, from trees to bodies of water. Use arrows to indicate the best views.

During this process, you'll want to investigate:
• Zoning
• Covenants
• Setbacks and height restrictions
• Building codes for snow, wind and seismic loads, and shoreline standards
• Accessibility for trucks and equipment
• Soils and drainage/perc tests
• Sewers or septic systems
• Electricity, gas, water, phone and cable TV

These factors may influence your home's design, site location—and they'll definitely have an impact on cost. Your Lindal consultant is an invaluable source of local information at this point.

Use a design notebook or file to expand your wish list and collect your thoughts—along with ideas from magazines and books.

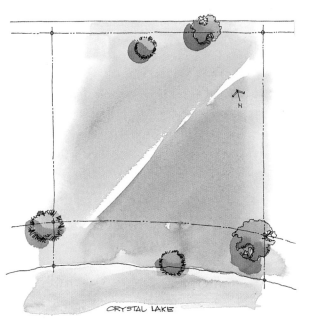

LAKE RIDGE ROAD

CRYSTAL LAKE

A picnic is a good way to get familiar with your site—including its best views, its unique microclimate, its natural strengths and drawbacks. Your local Lindal consultant will be glad to lend a hand—and bring the coffee.

"Our house lends itself well to its

Consider Architectural Style

You may already have a vivid image of your home's architectural personality. If not, a little style-setting now will provide a helpful framework for more detailed planning to come.

Arriving at an architectural style that's the ideal "fit" between client and site is the sort of thing an architect typically spends many hours working out. But in most cases, you can do it yourself with the help of your local Lindal consultant. You can create exactly the style you want from the ground up—or draw inspiration from our design library of Small Treasures, Contemporaries, Classics and Traditionals. Of course, you can also begin with an architect and bring your preliminary plans to us for completion. However you want to design your home, we're happy to be part of your team.

Budget-Wise Thinking

Building a Lindal gives you an unbeatable level of personal control over just where you put your money; budgets vary as much as people's priorities.

For example, if you're buying a lot with a knock-out view, you'll probably devote a significant percentage of your budget to the lot itself. And finishing costs can differ dramatically; obviously, granite counters cost more than formica, a whirlpool more than a tub.

Which brings us to an important reminder as you develop a budget: your Lindal package is only part of it. Be sure to include the cost of your property, excavation, landscaping, construction and interior finishing such as carpet, fixtures and cabinetry.

It's helpful to know early on what will affect costs: things such as your site and the ease of building on it; the size and design of your home (two-story homes, with daylight basements or second stories, tend to cost less per square foot than one-story homes). Construction costs also vary with location and the amount of "sweat equity" you're putting into your home.

Your local Lindal consultant can be a great help in making the most of your budget—advising where your dollars should go to give you the most home for your money and providing ballpark costs for construction in your area.

Write Your Own Program

Having studied your wants and needs, site and budget, an architect would develop a written program. You can too. Here's what you'll want to cover:

1) Overall Requirements
- Architectural style
- Number of stories
- Roof type
- Interior style (open and informal or contained and formal—or a combination?)
- Family size (big family, retirees?)

2) Individual Requirements
- The wants and needs of each family member

3) List of Rooms
- Including user(s), size and special needs

Congratulations!

You've accomplished the most critical part of the planning process—turning your dream into a list of specific requirements. By the end of this chapter, you'll be ready to turn those requirements into a working floorplan.

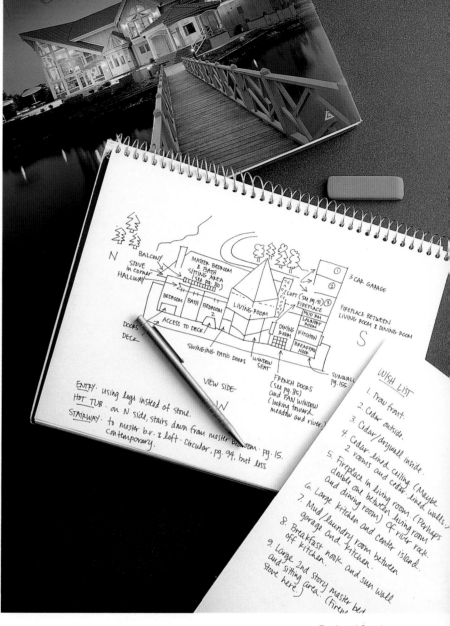

Fred and Sandy Bryant transformed their wish list into their own preliminary site and floorplan for their Lindal home in Sun Valley, Idaho.

location and seems to 'grow' out of the hill." Heinz and Edith Blessing, SC

Whether you're building on a steep hillside or a level lot, Lindal lets you develop an architectural style and floorplan that take advantage of your site. SC

The Powelson cedar clapboard residence opens up to a three-story view on the water side.

Thanks to Lindal's design flexibility and the openness of its post and beam construction, you can make the most of any site—and every view.

Enhancing the Lay of Your Land

You'll find that certain designs are naturals for a flat lot, while others allow you a 360-degree view from a hillside location. It's all a matter of choosing a home design and site orientation that make the most of your property's topography and view potential. Keep in mind that it makes more sense to adapt your home design to the land than vice versa; excavating and grading are expensive undertakings that can undermine the character of the site you fell in love with.

"Our Lindal has become a mecca for children, grandchildren and friends." Trudy Powelson, NJ

Flat Lot

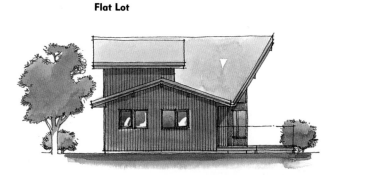

This home shows its private side to the street, with easy, level access to the main entrance.

Sloped Lot

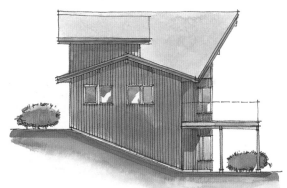

The beauty of a daylight basement on a sloping view lot: a spectacular outlook from both levels.

Steep Lot

If your lot is on a steep slope, consider Lindal pole construction.

Main Floor

SunWalls and a deck look out to the water from the main floor.

Upper Floor

Two bedrooms open to the upper floor balcony with water view.

The Powelson Residence, NJ
Bedrooms: 4
Bathrooms: 2 Full + 1 Half
Master bedroom on second floor
Total Area: 2444 sq. ft. excluding daylight basement
First Floor: 1444 sq. ft.
Other Floor: 1000 sq. ft.
Size: 48' x 35'
Entry: Back

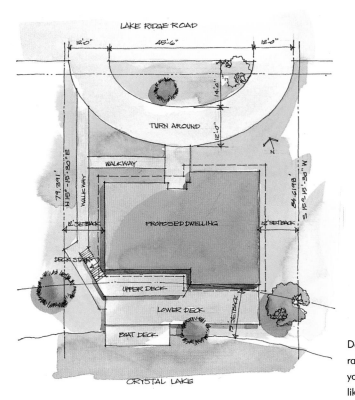

Document the topography of your land on your site plan, just like the Powelsons did.

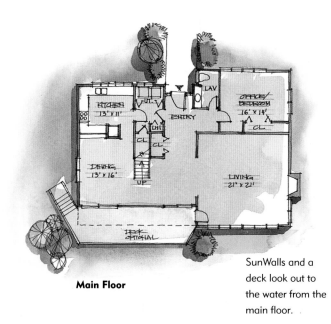

The Powelson streetfront exterior is designed for privacy.

Working with Nature

There's real joy—not to mention comfort and common sense—in a home that works with its natural environment. By taking advantage of your site's unique microclimate, you can harness the sun's free and renewable energy to heat and cool your home, take advantage of natural opportunities for ventilation, and build in protection from harsh winds and driving rains. Of course, functionality isn't the only reward of a site-sensitive design. The more a home lives in harmony with its natural surroundings, the more rewarding it is to your spirit and senses.

A wall of south-facing glass is essential to collect the free heat of the sun. This roof overhang is designed to admit the heat of the low winter sun and block the high summer rays in this cedar clapboard residence. NH

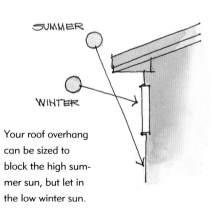

Your roof overhang can be sized to block the high summer sun, but let in the low winter sun.

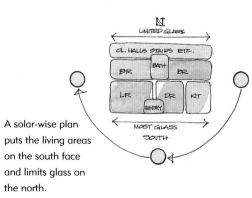

A solar-wise plan puts the living areas on the south face and limits glass on the north.

Passive Solar by Design

This Lindal original uses just about every passive solar technique in the book. Yet it was built for about the same price as a similarly sized, conventionally heated house in the same area. A well-designed solar home makes an attractive neighbor—and unlike its neighbors, most of its *heating needs are fueled by the sun. A wood-burning stove provides the rest. Insulating the house properly and picking up these passive solar techniques can save forty to ninety percent on your energy bills. More on the super-insulated home in chapter nine.*

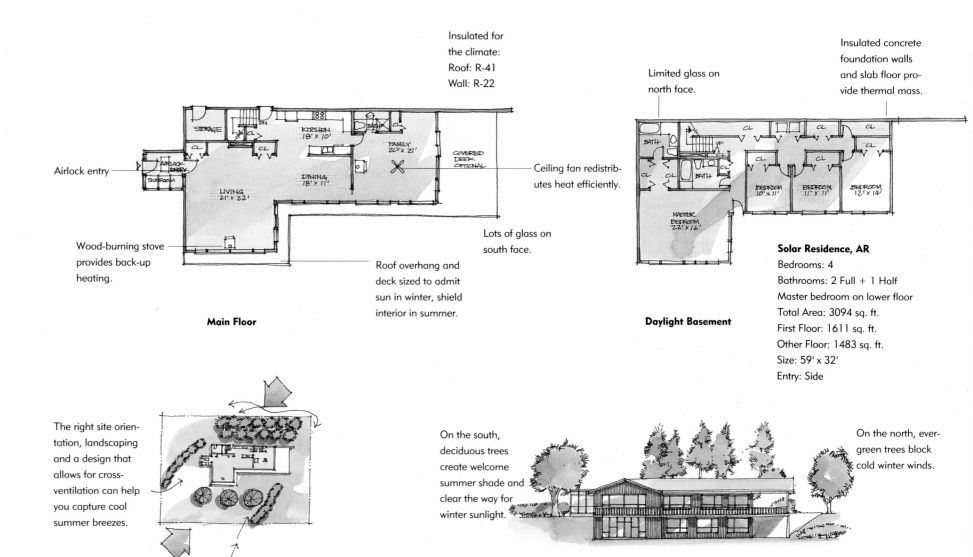

Insulated for the climate:
Roof: R-41
Wall: R-22

Limited glass on north face.

Insulated concrete foundation walls and slab floor provide thermal mass.

Airlock entry

Ceiling fan redistributes heat efficiently.

Wood-burning stove provides back-up heating.

Lots of glass on south face.

Roof overhang and deck sized to admit sun in winter, shield interior in summer.

Main Floor

Daylight Basement

Solar Residence, AR
Bedrooms: 4
Bathrooms: 2 Full + 1 Half
Master bedroom on lower floor
Total Area: 3094 sq. ft.
First Floor: 1611 sq. ft.
Other Floor: 1483 sq. ft.
Size: 59' x 32'
Entry: Side

The right site orientation, landscaping and a design that allows for cross-ventilation can help you capture cool summer breezes.

On the south, deciduous trees create welcome summer shade and clear the way for winter sunlight.

On the north, evergreen trees block cold winter winds.

If your aspirations for a home are bigger than your current budget, you

can plan a Lindal that starts small and grows later—right along with

your household. The secret is to plan for expansion from the beginning; it

The House that Grows

will affect the size of your lot and how your starter home is situated on it, how heating and cooling systems

are sized for cost-effective expansion, how plumbing and wiring are run,

and much more. The result? A home ready to expand whenever you are.

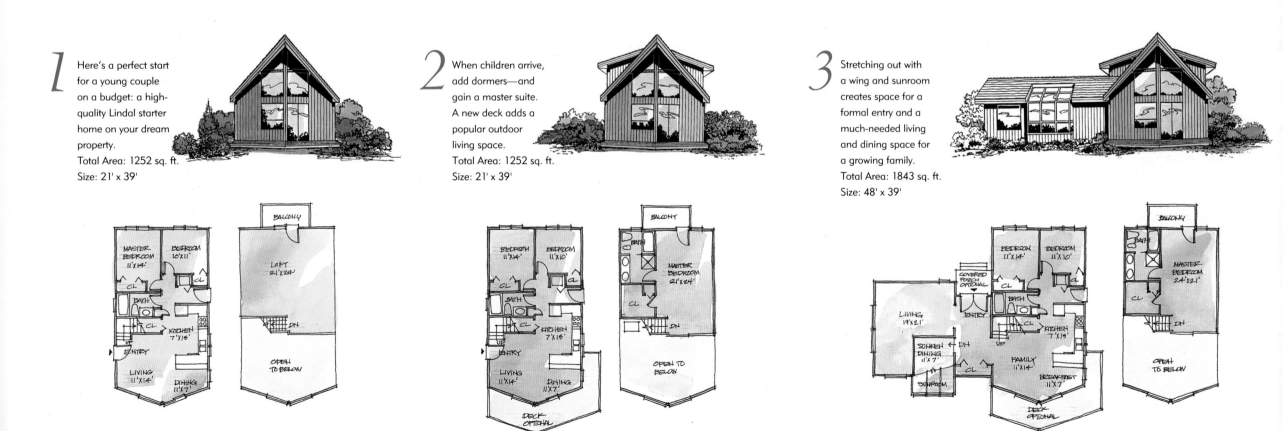

1 Here's a perfect start for a young couple on a budget: a high-quality Lindal starter home on your dream property.
Total Area: 1252 sq. ft.
Size: 21' x 39'

2 When children arrive, add dormers—and gain a master suite. A new deck adds a popular outdoor living space.
Total Area: 1252 sq. ft.
Size: 21' x 39'

3 Stretching out with a wing and sunroom creates space for a formal entry and a much-needed living and dining space for a growing family.
Total Area: 1843 sq. ft.
Size: 48' x 39'

"It is possible to take down walls for remodeling and reuse the same material without damage to the material." Homeowner, NY

We are very pleased with how difficult it is to tell new from old. Most people cannot believe that the house has been added onto." Homeowner, NY

A sunroom and formal dining room can easily be added at a later stage. WA

4

A second wing adds a roomy garage, work-shop, expanded utility room and decks.
Total Area: 2012 sq. ft.
Size: 77' x 39'

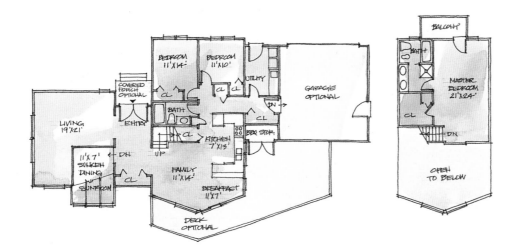

5

When the kids leave and stairs become a nuisance, move the master suite back to the main level by turn-ing the two original bedrooms into one. The loft becomes an ideal guest suite, home office or an appealing "nest" for children to come home to.
Total Area: 2012 sq. ft.
Size: 77' x 39'

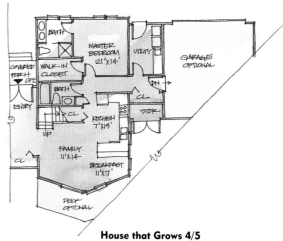

House that Grows 4/5
Bedrooms: 3/2
Bathrooms: 2
Master bedroom on second floor/main floor
Total Area: 2015 sq. ft.
First Floor: 1553 sq. ft.
Other Floor: 462 sq. ft.
Size: 77' x 39'
Entry: Back

"We've created a flow from our kitchen with its

sunroom and a step-up dining room. All rooms have French doors

Some homes just seem to "work" beautifully—and when they do, you

can be sure that a well-considered floorplan is underfoot. Basically, your

Creating a Floorplan that Flows

home's floorplan should make it easy and comfortable to go through the

motions of daily living. It should also create natural and complementary

relationships between rooms. Here's how to map out a master plan.

Traffic Patterns

Your main entry should allow you to enter any room in the house without passing through other rooms. Ideally, it will give guests easy access to the rooms you use most for entertaining.

The second entry should lead directly to the kitchen. If you can include a place between this entry and the kitchen to store coats and paraphernalia, you'll be glad you did.

Think about how each family member spends his or her day and walk through the plan you're considering. Any hitches? Give special attention to the type of daily chores that a good floorplan can make easier and more efficient—such as answering the door and carrying in groceries.

Activity Zones

The best-loved floorplans honor a household's basic activities—working, eating, sleeping and entertainment— by situating them in harmony with each other.

Ideally, the noisier zones, such as work and entertainment areas, are grouped together and well away from sleeping areas. In a residential neigh-borhood, you may want to locate your quiet zones toward the rear of your home—away from street noises and passersby. Of course, your site's ele-vation, view and surroundings will influence your decisions.

Wherever possible, each bedroom should also be buffered from other bed-rooms for the sake of privacy and quiet. Closets, staircases and bookshelves are effective sound barriers.

large island, to a step-down to the patio." Bob and Judy Newsome, VT

Kitchen

You'll want your kitchen to be convenient to the dining room, family room and outdoor patios and decks. If your cook likes to socialize with family and guests, consider opening the kitchen to other rooms. For much more information, see pages 142–145.

Dining Room

The best of both worlds: the formality of a private dining room and the open, airy feeling of the outdoors.

Bedrooms

To give you the furniture-arranging flexibility you need, bedrooms should have at least two walls uninterrupted by doors or low windows. Place closets between rooms to reduce noise transmission.

First Floor

Second Floor

Master Suite & Bath

Situate the door so you needn't cross the sleeping area to reach the bath or closets. Consider integrating the bath, closets and dressing area into a suite of separate but connected spaces. For more details, see pages 146–147.

Main Entry

Your main entry should be inviting, and lead directly into the formal living area. Yet it should also be well-defined and private enough that it doesn't put your entire house on view when the door is open. An entry closet is a daily convenience; so is easy access to other floors.

Second Entry

Life is easier when you have convenient access from your garage to your kitchen. If this entry is through a utility or mud room and has two doors, it creates an airlock— and you'll save on heating and air conditioning.

The Newsome Residence, VT

Bedrooms: 3 + Office
Bathrooms: 2 Full + 1 Three-quarter
Master bedroom on second floor
Total Area: 3243 sq. ft.
First Floor: 2507 sq. ft.
Other Floor: 736 sq. ft.
Size: 73' x 51'
Entry: Front
Specifications: Cedar clapboard

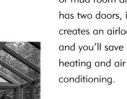

"Our house was built for entertaining."

These days, "what's cooking" in kitchens is far more than food preparation. The kitchen is the heart of many homes—an inviting place to socialize and entertain, a favorite place to make contact and make memories with your family, a nurturing spot you can settle into for a great meal or good conversation.

Creating Your Kitchen

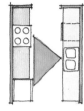

Corridor/Galley
Two parallel counters adapt well to an open kitchen concept. The drawback: traffic can interrupt the work triangle.

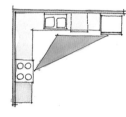

L-Shaped
Two walls at right angles form an "L" which supports an efficient triangle that lets traffic by without interrupting the cook.

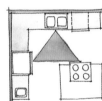

Island/Two Sinks
Islands work well in large "U" and "L" layouts; they minimize the distance of the work triangle in big kitchens. They can double as eating bars, too.

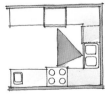

U-Shaped/Two Sinks
The ideal kitchen layout. The "dead end" eliminates traffic through the triangle. Two cooks can comfortably co-exist.

Kitchens that work share some underlying strengths: well thought-out traffic patterns; hard-working counters, islands and peninsulas; ample storage; low-maintenance materials; convenient clustering of work areas; and, increasingly in today's kitchens, work centers for more than one cook.

Rethinking the Classic Work Triangle
It used to be that all wise kitchen plans adhered to a formula which located sink, cooktop and refrigerator in a triangular arrangement. The goal? To reduce steps between these work centers—and keep extraneous traffic outside this inner sanctum. The total distance of the triangle's three sides would be no more than 22 feet, with no more than seven feet between each work area.

But the shapes of kitchens have changed as more families have more cooks in the kitchen. You may want to add a workstation outside the triangle. Or break out of the triangle altogether—with a common work island and wide aisles that let two cooks collaborate comfortably.

With lots of natural light, this kitchen is a joy to work in. WA

More kitchen ideas.
NJ and OR

Kitchen Tips:

🌲 Plan at least ten feet of counter space, excluding appliances.

🌲 The sink should have the most counter and storage space on both sides.

🌲 Make sure the sink access won't be blocked when the dishwasher door is open.

🌲 The refrigerator door should hinge away from the sink and cooktop.

🌲 Space between counters should be at least 36 to 48 inches—60 inches if cooking is often a two-person operation.

🌲 Consider a second sink for salad preparation or a wet bar outside the work triangle.

🌲 Since the oven is used less than the cooktop, it can be located outside the triangle. So can a microwave oven.

🌲 Plan for lots of storage—then double your estimate. You'll be glad you did.

🌲 Consider walk-in pantries, kitchen desks and "recycling centers"— are they for you?

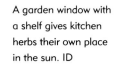

A garden window with a shelf gives kitchen herbs their own place in the sun. ID

Room for Living

Bobbi and Barry Freedman planned their kitchen to be a gathering place for family and friends. "With three active children, we use the kitchen for birthday celebrations, homework, assorted projects and many other events," they write. "It works well for all sizes of gatherings." That's because the Freedmans allowed plenty of room for folks to "cluster," whether they pull up a chair to the island or get together around the breakfast table.

Bobbi and Barry in the kitchen they designed themselves.

Don't forget a kitchen desk—the control center.

A drawer for utensils under the cooktop is extremely convenient.

Roll-out shelves make contents easily accessible.

How did we get along without a compactor?

"After four years of living in the house, we still have a special feeling every morning when we enter the kitchen. We would not change a thing." NJ

And on page 145, a totally different kitchen look in this North Carolina home.

The best bathrooms are an appealing combination of practical design and

pampering amenities. Most homes have two full bathrooms or more. And

at least one is designed to be a haven where you can shed the demands of Bathing Beauties

a busy world and soak up an environment that restores your energy and delights your senses. Good design—

the "bones" of your bathroom—is essential. So is budget awareness; costs

tend to run higher per square foot in this room than in any other.

Bathroom Tips:

♣ Locate bathrooms on outside walls to take advantage of natural light and ventilation. Or use a skylight; a ventilating one is both beautiful and functional.

♣ To maximize the sense of space, be lavish with windows. How about a skywall over the tub? A garden window for growing your own herbal aromatherapy? Or a full sunroom—for a bath as beautiful as all outdoors?

♣ Mirror small spaces to expand them visually and pick up light.

♣ Plan ample storage for grooming as well as for storing linens and bath supplies.

♣ To conserve water, choose low-volume toilets and reduced-flow showerheads.

♣ Double the usability of a bath by adding privacy walls or doors between fixtures. Two people can comfortably share a compartmentalized bath at the same time—a real blessing on busy mornings.

♣ Add amenities that will make your bath a private, personal bathing retreat: a whirlpool tub, second sink, separate shower and tub enclosures, a sit-down vanity—and, we repeat, plenty of storage.

♣ Pocket doors can save precious space.

Feel free to incorporate locally supplied items that are less practical for Lindal to provide—like glass block. VA

If your home is secluded, why not luxuriate in an all-glass environment while bathing? ON

"With the addition of sunrooms, we had the flexibility of showing to the fullest our best views." Homeowner, NC

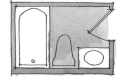

Full bathroom.

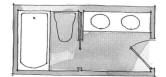

Full bath, compartmentalized, with two sinks and one entry.

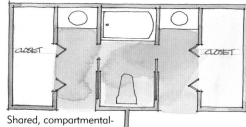

Shared, compartmentalized bath, with two sinks and two entries.

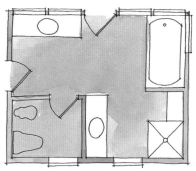

One-of-a-kind bath.

When you have a view you love, don't hesitate to enjoy it from every room. NC

Guest Suite

The high ceilings and charming fireplace in this guest suite provide a welcome retreat. NC

If you're planning for a home office or guest suite, you're not alone; these are two of the fastest-growing trends in home design. And although their

Offices & Guest Suites

end uses differ, one space can usually accommodate both. A self-sufficient oasis, complete with private bath, in a quiet part of the house with a sense of physical separation is best. A location just off a main entry is ideal. The idea is to create an independent suite that provides private space— whether it's for work or relaxing.

Office or Guest Suite Upstairs

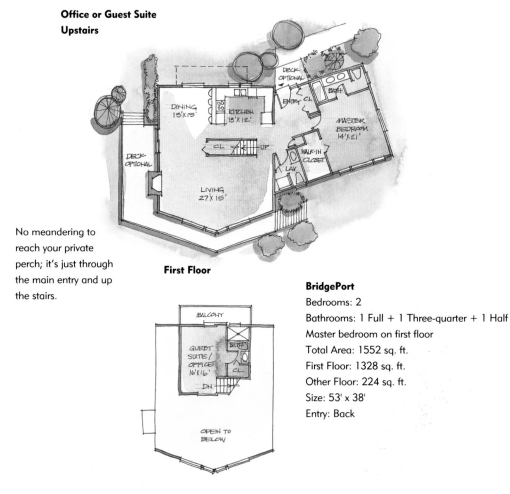

No meandering to reach your private perch; it's just through the main entry and up the stairs.

First Floor

Second Floor

BridgePort

Bedrooms: 2
Bathrooms: 1 Full + 1 Three-quarter + 1 Half
Master bedroom on first floor
Total Area: 1552 sq. ft.
First Floor: 1328 sq. ft.
Other Floor: 224 sq. ft.
Size: 53' x 38'
Entry: Back

Office and Guest Suite Off the Main Entry

This Lindal plan has everything— a home office and a guest suite.

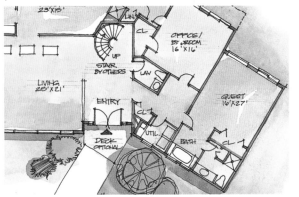

The ideal location— just off the entry.

For the full plan see the Green residence, page 38.

148

Storage is one thing you can never have too much of. Yet it's a surprisingly overlooked element of tailoring your home to your lifestyle. What's a

A Place for Everything

wine-lover's home without a wine cellar? A pool-player's rec room without a pool table? A computer enthusiast's study without a user-friendly desktop? Here's the chance of a lifetime to give your favorite hobbies and activities a home of their own—whether it's a walk-in pantry in the kitchen or an art studio in the loft.

"The clean lines of the beautiful wood beams, in contrast with the white walls, show off our art collection to perfection." Dick and Jo Feroe, VA

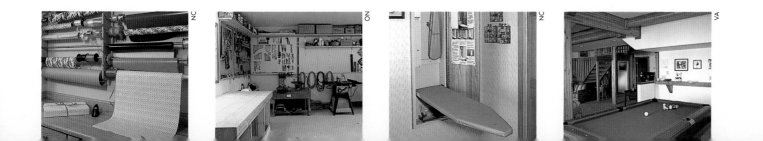

Who doesn't love an open, airy room with natural light and a wonderful

view? Wood-framed windows—finished like fine furniture—are key to

Designing with Glass

the architectural character and sensory delights of your Lindal home.

Besides opening up your home to garden charm and sweeping vistas,

they can "paint" your rooms with natural light and circulate fresh air

through your home.

Lindal's standard windows are available in clear Western red cedar or clear Douglas fir. Fir-framed windows have a thinner profile than cedar. All others are custom orders that require longer lead times. NC

Designing with windows is part art, part science—a balancing act that considers light, view, ventilation, energy efficiency and aesthetics. A few helpful tips:

• Decide what you want to achieve, both functionally and aesthetically, with the glass in your home. Where do you want privacy? A view? Where is ventilation important?

• Consider the character of light. Northern light is poetically diffuse, but north-facing windows are energy drains in winter. Eastern light is soft and pleasing. Southern light fuels passive solar gains—but plan for protection when heat comes on strong. Western light brings sunsets your way, but glare needs to be controlled in summer.

• The most pleasing, balanced room lighting comes from windows on two walls.

• Think about the visual impact of each window on the interior and exterior of your home.

• Stay true to a pattern of window style and placement that feels balanced.

• Windows have an enormous impact on the energy efficiency of your home. For more information, see page 256 or your local Lindal consultant.

A Palladian window, centered over gridded French doors and twin side windows, brings natural light into this living room—and frames a view of the greenery outside. VT

 Fixed Glass
Less expensive than opening windows, with the greatest energy efficiency and security of all. Available in a wide range of shapes and sizes. Western red cedar or Douglas fir.

 Awning
(with fixed glass) A long, horizontal window, hinged to open out from the bottom. Excellent screened ventilation and good rain protection when open. Cedar or fir.

 Casement
A tall, vertical window hinged on one side to open like a door. Excellent screened ventilation. Cedar or fir.

 Single Hung
A traditional window; the bottom half slides up to open. Optional grids available. Custom order. Fir.

 **Double Hung**
Another traditional. Upper and lower halves slide independently. Optional grids available. Custom order. Fir.

 **Slider**
This window opens just like a sliding glass door. Custom order. Fir.

 **Jalousies**
Wood and glass louvers open for ventilation and offer protection from rain. Low in energy efficiency and security. Popular in tropical climates. Cedar.

 **Dream Windows**
You can custom-order windows in every shape and size, including Palladians (fans), half-rounds, bows, bays, rounds and octagons. Fir.

Picture windows frame the view, while French doors lead to the patio. Conrad residence, CA

Light, Views & Ventilation

When it comes to bringing natural light, fresh air and the great outdoors

into your Lindal, windows are only the beginning. Take a look at what

you can do with wood-framed doors, skylights and garden windows.

Designing with Doors

Glass doors in all their appealing variety—sliding glass doors, swinging patio doors, French doors and store doors—are an inviting way to extend living and entertaining out of doors. They also make charming interior entries to a sunroom, atrium or indoor pool.

Skylights (Fixed and Opening)

Consider a skylight over your main entry, lighting up a long corridor or small bathroom, over a stairwell— anywhere you want to add drama, light and ventilation.

Garden Windows

You can cultivate a little greenhouse with a garden window in your kitchen or bathroom. This wood-framed, three-dimensional window has a shelf that gives plants a place in the sun. Vented side panels open to catch summer breezes.

The Quality Is Clear

Whatever eye-catching openings you choose for your Lindal, you'll find they're tops in energy efficiency and wood-framed for visual richness and warmth. Naturally, they are a beautiful complement to the cedar exterior of any Lindal home. More information on page 256.

Four Velux® roof windows grace this charming bedroom. IL

This kitchen enjoys both a skylight and a garden window. OR

Swinging patio doors open from the bedroom to the deck. OR

As you place windows into your plan, think about air flow. Well-designed circulation can do wonders for the comfort of your home.

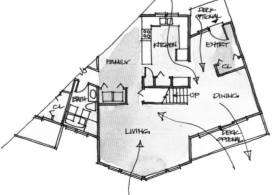

Access to the deck is easy with sliding glass doors. TN

"We love the daily and seasonal play of sunlight and moonlight

that enter the house through the ample windows and skylights." Homeowner, MD

It's no surprise that sunrooms, with their stunning looks, quality crafts-

manship and sophisticated engineering, are incorporated into so many

Lindal homes these days. But we've recently introduced a host of new

related products that may also pique your interest. Let your Lindal

consultant be your guide to all the exciting options now available.

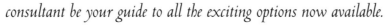

SunRooms, etc.

Back-to-Back
SunRoom. ON

"Our sunroom is of exceptional quality. It's added great

beauty and enjoyment from sunrise to sunset." Greg and Lydia LaHaie, OR

SunCurve: Cedar. ON

SunSpace: Aluminum. MD

SkyWall. WA

SunCrescent. MI

SunCanopy. CT

GardenRoom. VA

Arborvitae or tree of life: the botanical classification of Western red cedar attests to its rare and wondrous qualities as a building material.

Outdoor Living

You gain a lot more than square feet when you extend your living space outdoors with a deck or porch. These are the places memories are made —where leisurely days and starlit nights are spent relaxing and entertaining. Lindal's outdoor living spaces combine top quality with top specifications—so there's none of the squeaking or bouncing so common in lesser-built options.

You can design Lindal decks to any size or configuration; let your needs and the topography of your site be your guides. Multi-level decks can provide separate areas of activity and visual interest. Sturdy railings add a finished look, and for safety be sure to build railings according to Lindal plans and details. Built-in seating makes great sense, too.

A screened-in porch is a welcome relief in hot climates where you want to let in cool breezes and keep out insects. These are relaxing retreats that conjure up visions of wicker chairs and iced tea.

Tips for Decking Out

🌲 For the ultimate in beauty and practicality, choose decking, railing and undercarriage in Western red cedar; it resists rot and insects.

🌲 Lindal deck planks are a solid 2" thick to protect against warping and twisting—and prevent the bounce so common in lesser-built decks.

🌲 Sliding glass or patio doors make it a breeze to serve meals outdoors.

🌲 Plan ahead for a hot tub; decide where it will be located and add reinforcement and support below the deck according to the tub manufacturer's instructions.

🌲 Consider building seating and large planters into your deck design.

🌲 At night, lighting can turn a deck into a romantic haven. It's an important safety consideration, too.

Cedar Simple Rail

Cedar 2 x 2 Rail

Cedar Seat Rail

"Living in our Lindal is like being on vacation every day." David and Cathy Osterman, TN

When summer comes to Thunder Bay, the Robinsons move to their outdoor living room. ON

A multi-level deck
extends living out
of doors. BC

Rick and Bobbi Freitag
designed a roomy
wraparound deck. WI

Custom-designed
seating takes advan-
tage of the valley
view. CA

An airy screened
porch with a view of
Georgian Bay. ON

No stairs at
front entry.

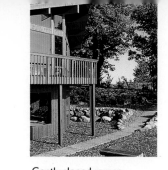

Gently sloped ramps
lead to the back of
the house.

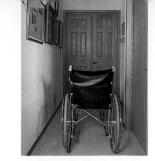

Halls should be
over 40" wide and
doors 36".

There's a final and important consideration before you begin to draw

your dream home. Because with a little forethought now, you can ensure

that you won't be forced to move out of it later on. Universal Design, as

the industry calls it, applies "barrier-free" thinking to the practicalities of   # ♿ Life Without Barriers

getting around the house in a wheelchair. The Lindal home of Vernon and Toodie Schultz is living proof that

you needn't sacrifice beauty for the liberating functionality of Universal

Design. And the added effort and expense are minimal when you incor-

porate it into your home plans from the start. It's a small price for a

home that will last you a lifetime.

Schultz Residence, MN
The Schultzes modified
the CliffSide. For the
original plan, see
page 193.

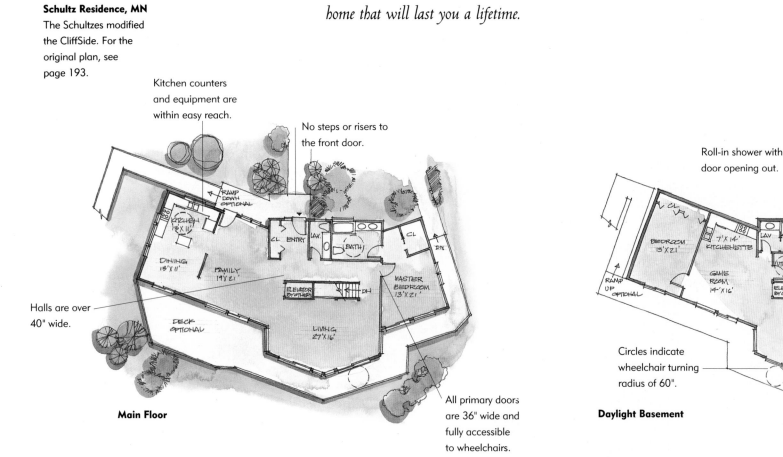

Kitchen counters
and equipment are
within easy reach.

No steps or risers to
the front door.

Halls are over
40" wide.

Main Floor

All primary doors
are 36" wide and
fully accessible
to wheelchairs.

Roll-in shower with
door opening out.

Handrails added to
bathrooms.

Circles indicate
wheelchair turning
radius of 60".

Daylight Basement

Vernon's mother
has a spacious
barrier-free apart-
ment to herself.

"I'd remind anyone
who plans to live to
a ripe old age in
their Lindal home to
think long and hard
about a barrier-free
living environment."

Lever-action door
handles replace
doorknobs.

Reinforce walls now
to accommodate
grab bars later.

"Lindal's post and beam construction was absolutely perfect for building a barrier-free home fully accessible

to my wheelchair friends, ninety-year-old mother and, who knows, maybe ourselves in a few years." Vernon Schultz, MN

Now, Draw Your Dream

With a chapter full of planning ideas and your site plan and written

program as handy references, you're ready to design your home. We sug-

gest you use a trick of the architect's trade: draw a "bubble" for every

major living space, and watch your home's layout take shape as you

arrange and rearrange them into a plan that works.

An exterior view of
the front of this North
Carolina home is
shown on page 98.

**Step One: Start with a
"Bubble" Design**
Draw bubbles for all major living
spaces, and identify each with a letter
("K" for kitchen, "B" for bedroom, and
so on). Now have some fun with them.
Make loose sketches and don't worry
about the accuracy of scale; the spatial
relationships between rooms are what
matter most now.

Using bubbles to sketch the relationship between spaces will help you
choose the ideal locations for each
room. For example, if you want your
kitchen to capture the morning sun,
place it to the east.

Step Two: A Loose Interpretation
When you have a clear idea of how your
rooms should interrelate, you're ready
to let those circles take the shape of
actual rooms.

Step Three: A Line Drawing
Now you can link the rooms in a preliminary line drawing of your floorplan. You can even include interior
doorways, major windows, decks—as
much detail as you have at this point.

**Step Four: Bring Scale into
the Picture**
Discover how gratifying it is to bring
your preliminary floorplan into scale
with the indispensable tools and tips
from your Home Planning Kit (available at your local Lindal dealership).

Can We Help?
You may enjoy the design process so
much that you want to do it all yourself—and with these guidelines, you
can. But remember that, at any point
along the way, you can turn the project
over to your local Lindal consultant for
design support and a complimentary
feasibility and cost analysis. And of
course, you just may find a dream
plan—or one that's close to it—in the
design library ahead.

1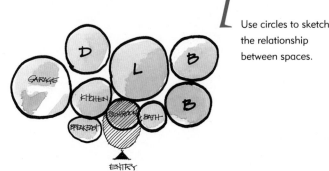

Use circles to sketch
the relationship
between spaces.

2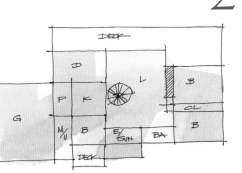

Now reshape those
circles into "rooms."

3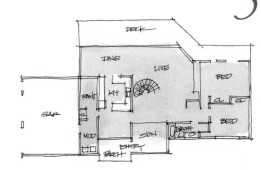

Link the rooms into a
preliminary floorplan.

Clerestory windows bathe the kitchen in natural light from above.

A wide deck extends living to the outdoors.

From the second floor, there's a bird's-eye view of the dining room.

4 Bring your plan on-site and into scale.

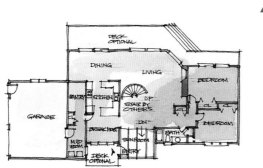

Note: Second floor not shown.

plans

Lindal plans are the ultimate in livability and style—the culmination of decades of design and home-building experience. Most Lindal originals are inspired by the plans in this design library, and they can easily be modified to suit the most personal wants and needs. Add a window or a wing. Expand a room. Change the roofline; add a sunroom. Your local Lindal dealership can provide assistance anytime during your planning process, and whenever you'd like a complimentary feasibility and cost analysis of your plan. Or, if you prefer, just give your Lindal consultant your wish list—and let us do the work.

Plans Index

	Page Number	First Floor Sq. Ft.	Other Floor Sq. Ft.	Total Sq. Ft.	Number of Floors	Overall Size	Number of Bedrooms	Number of Baths	Master Bedroom on Floor
Inspirations									
Casa Islena	20	3962	2780	6742	2	116x74	4+	3+2	1
An Enlightened Log Home	24	2490		2490	1	99x50	2+	2	1
Modern Outlook	26	1242	1263	2505	2	65x40	3	2 1/2	2
Stone House Revival	28	3359	1396	4755	2	79x66	4+	1+2	2
Timeless Treasures	30	1714	684	2398	2	64x34	3+	2+2	1
Northwest Light	32	1815	950	2765	2	67x34	3+	3 1/2	1
Neighborly by Design	33	1661	911	2572	2	48x59	4	2+2	2
Dream Ranch	34	3180	985	4165	2	111x58	3+	3+2	1
Pine Hill Farm	36	2123	856	2979	2	70x51	3+	2 1/2	2
Woodland Retreat	38	3256	548	3804	2	104x50	3	3+2	2
Hilltop Oasis	40	1939	893	2832	2	84x40	2+	2+2	1
Home Planning Ideas									
Powelson Residence	135	1444	1000	2444	2	48x35	4	2 1/2	2
Solar Residence	137	1611	1483	3094	2	59x32	4	2 1/2	1
House that Grows #4/#5	139	1553	462	2015	2	77x39	3/2	2	2/1
Newsome Residence	141	2507	736	3243	2	73x51	3+	2+1	2
Schultz Residence/ CliffSide	158	1723	1757	3480	2	73x41	3	1+2	1
Small Treasures									
Contempo Prow									
Hudson	169	1173		1173	1	32x39	2	1	1
Fraser	169	1068	263	1331	2	37x32	3	2	2
Columbia	170	1485	351	1836	2	43x39	3	3	1
St. Lawrence	170	1517	372	1889	2	43x39	3	2	2
Chalet									
Vail	171	608	566	1174	2	21x29	2	1 1/2	2
Aspen	171	806	383	1189	2	28x30	2+	1	1
Stowe	172	833	461	1294	2	25x36	2	2	2
Tahoe	172	1041	555	1596	2	27x40	3	2	2
Prow									
Coronado	173	689	331	1020	2	21x34	2	2	2
Chesapeake	173	1093	795	1888	2	29x42	3	2	2
Catalina	174	790	462	1252	2	21x39	2+	1	1
Greenbriar	174	1019	607	1626	2	27x40	3	2	2
Capistrano	175	1461	844	2305	2	32x48	3	2 1/2	1
Niagara	175	507	261	768	2	21x26	1+	1	1
Haliburton	176	1360	683	2043	2	37x47	2	1 3/4	2
Shenandoah	177	1467	1022	2489	2	39x42	3	3	2

	Page Number	First Floor Sq. Ft.	Other Floor Sq. Ft.	Total Sq. Ft.	Number of Floors	Overall Size	Number of Bedrooms	Number of Baths	Master Bedroom on Floor
Summit									
Teton	179	1079	403	1482	2	32x36	3	2	2
Whitney	180	917	306	1223	2	32x31	2	2	2
Sierra	180	912	316	1228	2	27x37	3	2	2
Shasta	181	1109	385	1494	2	32x37	2	2	2
Olympic	181	1346	344	1690	2	43x35	3	2	2
View									
Malibu	182	907		907	1	27x34	2	1	1
Riviera	182	1093		1093	1	29x41	3	2	1
Capri I	183	720		720	1	27x27	2	1	1
Capri II	183	1025		1025	1	46x27	3	2	1
Capri III	183	1113		1113	1	54x27	3	2	1
Waikiki I w/o basement	184	1184		1184	1	32x37	2	1 3/4	1
Waikiki II w/basement	184	1153	591	1744	2	32x37	3	2 3/4	1
Panorama									
Acapulco	185	999	227	1226	2	37x26	3	2	1
Monaco I & II	185	1337	227	1564	2	43x37	3+	1 3/4	1
Gambrel									
Concord	186	667	628	1295	2	21x31	3	2	2
Lexington	186	827	788	1615	2	27x31	3	1 1/2	2
Pole									
Kona	187	1376		1376	1	37x37	3	2	1
Sausalito	187	2304		2304	1	48x48	4	2	1
Contemporary									
Contempo Prow Star									
BaySide	188	1514		1514	1	54x35	3	2	1
SeaSide	188	1553		1553	1	59x32	2	2	1
LakeSide	189	1624		1624	1	57x33	3	2	1
CapeSide	189	1758		1758	1	73x39	3	2	1
ParkSide	190	1833		1833	1	67x41	2	1 3/4	1
Contempo Prow Star Variations									
OceanSide	191	2062		2062	1	66x40	3	2	1
HillSide	192	877	1350	2227	2	55x32	3	3 1/2	1
CliffSide	193	1723	1757	3480	2	73x41	3	2 1/2	1
RiverSide	194	1927	368	2295	2	64x54	3+	2	1
Contempo Prow Star: Building Up									
ValleySide	195	1805	179	1984	2	64x39	2+	1 3/4	1
CountrySide	196	1842	1341	3183	2	69x44	4	3 1/2	2

	Page Number	First Floor Sq. Ft.	Other Floor Sq. Ft.	Total Sq. Ft.	Number of Floors	Overall Size	Number of Bedrooms	Number of Baths	Master Bedroom on Floor
Chalet Star									
RoseHill	197	1163	297	1460	2	45x31	3	2	2
FernHill	198	1104	395	1499	2	40x31	2	2	2
GlenHill	199	1287	378	1665	2	51x30	3	2	2
FairHill	200	1641	547	2188	2	56x30	3	2	2
Prow Star									
BayVista	201	1187	200	1387	2	53x27	1+	2	1
FairVista	202	1375	311	1686	2	54x34	2	2 1/2	1
SkyVista	203	1255	489	1744	2	41x41	3	2	2
ValleyVista	204	1323	433	1756	2	49x35	3	2	2
CascadeVista	205	1551	270	1821	2	59x32	2+	2	1
SeaVista	206	1454	384	1838	2	60x36	3	2	2
ViewVista	207	1920		1920	1	67x43	1	1 1/2	1
LakeVista	208	1457	560	2017	2	47x37	2	1 3/4	2
RiverVista	209	1672	351	2023	2	59x36	3	3	2
MountainVista	210	1992	284	2276	2	71x38	2+	2	1
BrookVista	211	1026	1378	2404	2	59x31	3	2 1/2	1
Prow Star with Two-Story Wings									
WoodLawn	212	1278	764	2042	2	46x38	3	2 1/2	2
WoodGate	213	1507	1032	2539	2	49x38	4	2 1/2	2
Prow Star with One & Two-Story Wings									
WoodLand	214	1641	910	2551	2	57x36	4	3 1/2	2
WoodHaven	215	2189	947	3136	2	69x47	4	3	2
Summit Star									
BridgePort	148	1328	224	1552	2	53x38	2	1+2	1
NewPort	216	1740	324	2064	2	65x38	3	2 1/2	1
WestPort	217	1662	420	2082	2	56x39	3	3	1
Classic									
Ranch									
Ponderosa	218	1500		1500	1	43x49	3	2	1
Silverado	219	2700		2700	1	66x56	3	2	1
Split Level									
Tuscany	220	1035	581	1616	2	37x31	3+	2	2
Bavaria	221	1403	764	2167	2	43x44	2+	2 3/4	2
College									
Harvard	222	1535	858	2393	2	53x43	3+	2 1/2	2
Princeton	223	2040	1017	3057	2	64x48	4	2 1/2	2

	Page	First Floor Sq. Ft.	Other Floor Sq. Ft.	Total Sq. Ft.	Number of Floors	Overall Size	Number of Bedrooms	Number of Baths	Master Bedroom on Floor
Pavilion									
Starlight	224	2152	872	3024	2	69x46	4	2 1/2	1
Stargazer	225	2181	1408	3589	2	73x49	4+	2 1/2	2
Executive									
Georgetown	226	1622	604	2226	2	64x32	3+	1+2	1
Scarsdale	227	2466	933	3399	2	68x43	4+	3 1/2	1
City									
Hillsborough	228	998	728	1726	2	35x33	3+	2 1/2	2
Westchester	229	1447	996	2443	2	43x38	4	3	2
Signature									
Landmark	230	1255	682	1937	2	43x32	3+	2	2
Hallmark	231	1548	798	2346	2	50x35	3+	2 1/2	1
Designer									
Sundowner	232	1429	591	2020	2	51x32	3	2	2
Sunburst	233	1906	636	2542	2	60x37	3	2	2
Traditional									
Cape									
Cape Breton	234	1863	670	2533	2	62x34	3	2 3/4	1
Tudor									
Cotswold	235	1340	1735	3075	2	54x43	4+	2 1/2	2
Heritage									
Hancock	236	981	597	1578	2	37x30	3	2	2
Yorktown	237	1334	817	2151	2	47x34	3+	2 3/4	2
Colonial									
Mayflower	238	1392	515	1907	2	48x35	3	2	2
New England									
Patriot	239	1075	958	2033	2	40x28	3	2	1
Whaler	240	1184	1143	2327	2	37x32	4	2 1/2	2
Liberty									
Independence	241	938	676	1614	2	42x23	3+	2	1
Revere	242	1231	941	2172	2	45x27	3+	3	2
Farmhouse									
Pioneer	243	1067	800	1867	2	40x27	3	2 1/2	1

Note: The + symbol indicates one or more bonus rooms such as a media room, library, family room or office.

"Dormer" indicates that the sloped roof has been raised to provide headroom at outside walls, increasing usable floor space substantially. ON

Reading The Plans

Please note: while our home photos provide great ideas, please do not rely on them for exact specifications. After all, one of the beauties of Lindal is that our homeowners can, and do, modify plans to create their own original. So when you create yours it's important to consult your plans and the current General Specification Sheet.

• Plans and photos often show optional features, such as garages, decks, porches, skylights, and sunrooms, which can be ordered from Lindal.

• Plans and photos sometimes show features not supplied by Lindal, such as appliances, fixtures, chimneys, fireplaces, wood stoves, shelving, etc.

• Photos sometimes show Lindal-supplied materials used differently than depicted in the authorized Lindal plans—e.g., deck railing. Be sure to comply with your local building code.

Decks, porches and garages are optional.

In Contemporary Style Series "Star" indicates that the models in a series have wings. ON

Series:
Homes sharing common features.

Model:
Variations of homes in a series.

Square Footage:
Includes main living area and loft, but excludes optional features such as garages, decks, porches, sunrooms, etc.

Dimensions:
Longest and widest points, excluding optional features. Rounded up and down to the closest foot.

Photo Reference:
Helps you find representative photos of homes in the series.

Architectural style:
Small Treasures, Contemporary, Classic and Traditional.

Solid arrow indicates main entry.

Indicates open rail.

Dimensions of the master bedroom suite include bathroom and closets.

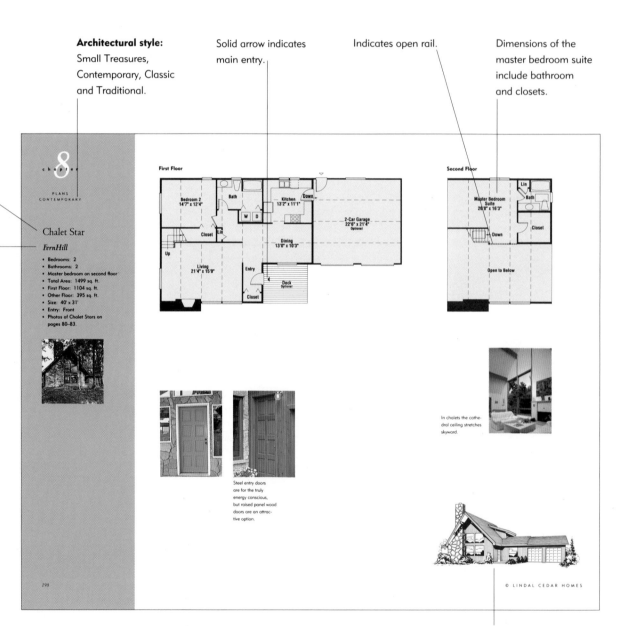

8

chapter

PLANS
CONTEMPORARY

Chalet Star

FernHill

• Bedrooms: 2
• Bathrooms: 2
• Master bedroom on second floor
• Total Area: 1499 sq. ft.
• First Floor: 1104 sq. ft.
• Other Floor: 395 sq. ft.
• Size: 40 x 31
• Entry: Front
• Photos of Chalet Stars on pages 80–83.

First Floor

Bedroom 2
14'7" x 12'4"

Bath

Kitchen
13'2" x 11'1"

Down

Closet

W D

2-Car Garage
22'6" x 21'4"
Optional

Dining
13'0" x 10'3"

Up

Living
21'4" x 15'0"

Entry

Deck
Optional

Closet

Second Floor

Lin

Master Bedroom
Suite
28'6" x 16'3"

Bath

Closet

Down

Open to Below

In chalets the cathedral ceiling stretches skyward.

Steel entry doors are for the truly energy conscious, but raised panel wood doors are an attractive option.

© LINDAL CEDAR HOMES

An artist's perspective of the home.

Topknot—like a dormer—adds headroom and usable floor space upstairs—but is usually centered over the ridge. HI

Any Lindal plan can be built on a daylight or full basement, over a crawl space, on a slab or on a permanent wood foundation. In some plans, an optional basement stair detail is provided, but all plans can be converted to accommodate them. Design tip: with basements, stack your stairs. SC

4/12: Low pitch.

8/12: A higher pitch.

Counters, appliances and fixtures are a suggestion for placement. They are not supplied by Lindal.

Parallel broken lines inside the plan indicate beams overhead.

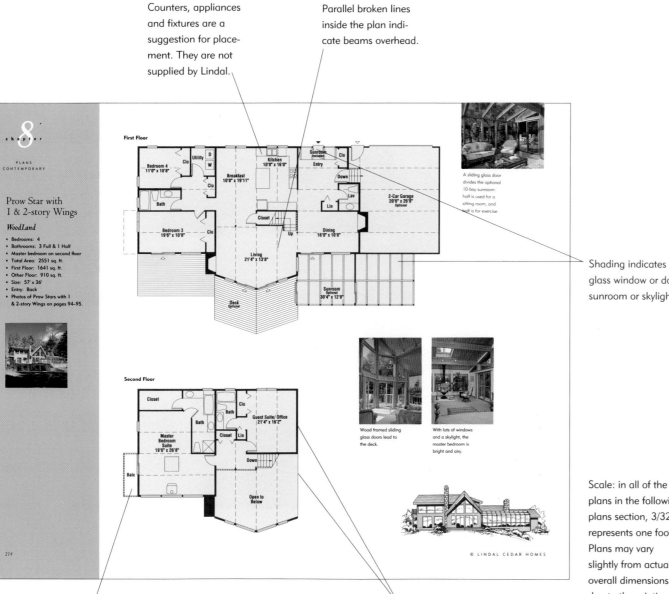

8'
chapter

PLANS
CONTEMPORARY

Prow Star with 1 & 2-story Wings

WoodLand

- Bedrooms: 4
- Bathrooms: 3 Full & 1 Half
- Master bedroom on second floor
- Total Area: 2551 sq. ft.
- First Floor: 1641 sq. ft.
- Other Floor: 910 sq. ft.
- Size: 57' x 36'
- Entry: Back
- Photos of Prow Stars with 1 & 2-story Wings on pages 94-95.

First Floor

Bedroom 4 11'0" x 10'8"
Utility
Breakfast 10'8" x 19'11"
Kitchen 10'8" x 16'0"
Sunroom (included) 10'8" x 16'0"
Entry
Down
Bath
Law
2-Car Garage 20'6" x 26'8" Optional
Bedroom 3 19'6" x 10'8"
Closet
Up
Dining 16'0" x 10'8"
Living 21'4" x 13'8"
Sunroom Optional 30'4" x 12'8"
Deck Optional

A sliding glass door divides the optional 10-bay sunroom: half is used for a sitting room, and half is for exercise.

Shading indicates glass window or door, sunroom or skylight.

Second Floor

Closet
Clo
Bath
Bath
Guest Suite/ Office 21'4" x 16'2"
Master Bedroom Suite 19'6" x 26'8"
Closet
Lin
Down
Balc
Open to Below

Wood framed sliding glass doors lead to the deck.

With lots of windows and a skylight, the master bedroom is bright and airy.

© LINDAL CEDAR HOMES

Sunrooms and skylights are optional unless otherwise stated. CA

12/12: The steepest pitch.

Gambrel: Two pitches.

Second floor balconies are included.

In two-story homes, wide dark lines in the perimeter of the second floor indicate the outside walls are full height; thinner, lighter lines indicate the roof is sloped. ON

Scale: in all of the plans in the following plans section, 3/32" represents one foot. Plans may vary slightly from actual overall dimensions due to the printing process.

Hip: A four-sided roof.

Plan It Your Way

The process of planning a dream home should be just as personal as the results. And at Lindal, it is. You can have just as much—or just as little—involvement as you wish in the planning process.

Personalizing a Lakeside Retreat
Stan and Lois Grant's New Hampshire lakeside home is a beautiful example of how easy it is to make a Lindal plan your own.

The Grants loved Lindal's Sunburst, but they wanted a larger floorplan. And instead of a sunroom, Stan preferred a solid roof over the entry and an enclosed sun porch with windows that open to the lake. He modified their plan accordingly. The result? "We ended up with a real lake home." Stan Grant says. "Maybe when I retire, I can sign on with you as a designer."

Choose a Proven Success.
Some homeowners wouldn't change a thing about their favorite Lindal plan. So if you prefer the convenience of a stock plan, you've come to the right place; Lindal offers the widest selection of cedar home styles and floorplans in the world.

Personalize Your Favorite Plan.
We make it easy for you to modify your favorite Lindal plan according to your personal wants and needs. If you like the idea of really getting involved in the planning, you'll love how easy our Home Planning Kit—and your local Lindal consultant—make the process.

Or Design Your Original from the Ground Up.
More and more people who are designing their own homes or working with architects come to Lindal for the quality materials and craftsmanship they just can't get anywhere else. We're delighted to be part of your team. CA

"You will love the view from my porch, but I get to sit in the rocking chair." Stan Grant, NH

"Our home is the envy of the neighborhood." Stan and Lois Grant, NH

Contempo Prow

Hudson

- Bedrooms: 2
- Bathrooms: 1
- Total Area: 1173 sq. ft.
- Size: 32' x 39'
- Entry: Side
- Photos of Contempo Prows on pages 46–47.

Master Bedroom
16'0" x 13'6"

Clo

Clo

Bedroom 2
16'0" x 10'0"

Bath

Lin

Closet

D **W**

Entry

Kitchen
12'8" x 8'4"

Living
19'4" x 15'6"

Dining
12'8" x 12'5"

Deck
Optional

Top Knot

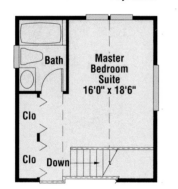

Bath

Master Bedroom Suite
16'0" x 18'6"

Clo

Clo

Down

First Floor

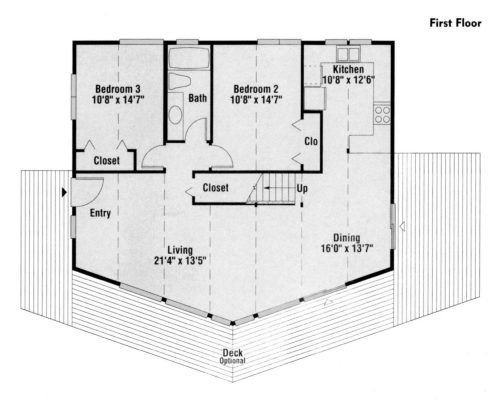

Bedroom 3
10'8" x 14'7"

Bath

Bedroom 2
10'8" x 14'7"

Kitchen
10'8" x 12'6"

Closet

Closet

Clo

Up

Entry

Living
21'4" x 13'5"

Dining
16'0" x 13'7"

Deck
Optional

Fraser

- Bedrooms: 3
- Bathrooms: 2
- Master bedroom on second floor
- Total Area: 1331 sq. ft.
- First Floor: 1068 sq. ft.
- Other Floor: 263 sq. ft.
- Size: 37' x 32'
- Entry: Side
- Photos of Contempo Prows on pages 46–47.

PLANS
SMALL TREASURES

Contempo Prow

Columbia

- Bedrooms: 3
- Bathrooms: 3
- Master bedroom on first floor
- Total Area: 1836 sq. ft.
- First Floor: 1485 sq. ft.
- Other Floor: 351 sq. ft.
- Size: 43' x 39'
- Entry: Back
- Photos of Contempo Prows
  on pages 46–47.

St. Lawrence

- Bedrooms: 3
- Bathrooms: 2
- Master bedroom on second floor
- Total Area: 1889 sq. ft.
- First Floor: 1517 sq. ft.
- Other Floor: 372 sq. ft.
- Size: 43' x 39'
- Entry: Side
- Photos of Contempo Prows
  on pages 46–47.

First Floor

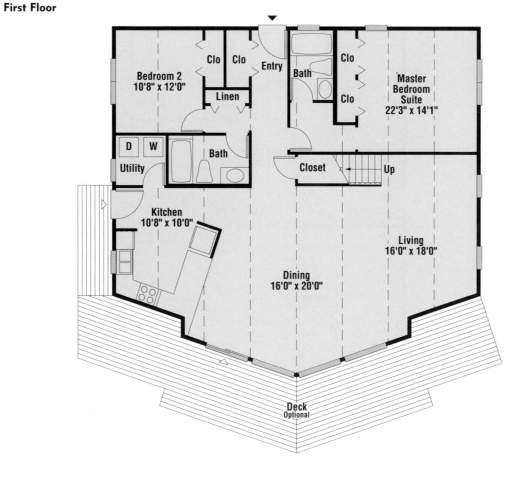

Bedroom 2
10'8" x 12'0"

Clo Clo Entry Bath Clo

Master
Bedroom
Suite
22'3" x 14'1"

Linen Clo

D W Bath

Utility

Kitchen
10'8" x 10'0"

Closet Up

Living
16'0" x 18'0"

Dining
16'0" x 20'0"

Deck
Optional

Top Knot

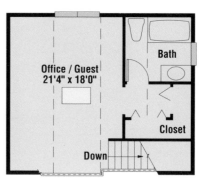

Office / Guest
21'4" x 18'0"

Bath

Closet

Down

The owners opted
for an open riser
staircase.

First Floor

Kitchen
10'8" x 14'7"

Bath

Clo

Bedroom 3
10'8" x 14'7"

Bedroom 2
10'8" x 18'4"

D W

Clo

Up Linen

Closet

Entry

Dining
10'8" x 19'2"

Living
32'0" x 20'10"

Deck
Optional

Top Knot

Master
Bedroom
Suite
21'4" x 18'6"

Bath

Down Clo

For more shelter from
tropical sun and rain,
the homeowners
widened the roof
overhang.

A dormer increases usable living space on the second floor in homes with sloped side walls.

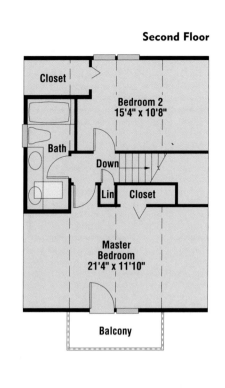

Closet

Bedroom 2
15'4" x 10'8"

Bath

Down

Lin | Closet

Master Bedroom
21'4" x 11'10"

Balcony

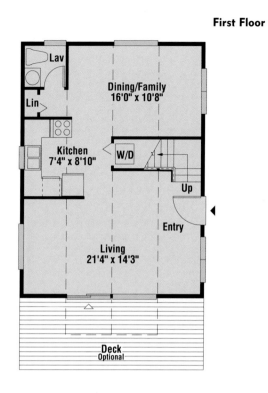

Lav

Lin

Dining/Family
16'0" x 10'8"

Kitchen
7'4" x 8'10"

W/D

Up

Entry

Living
21'4" x 14'3"

Deck
Optional

Chalet

Vail

- Bedrooms: 2
- Bathrooms: 1 Full & 1 Half
- Master bedroom on second floor
- Total Area: 1174 sq. ft.
- First Floor: 608 sq. ft.
- Other Floor: 566 sq. ft.
- Size: 21' x 29'
- Entry: Side
- Photos of Chalets on pages 48–49.

Second Floor

First Floor

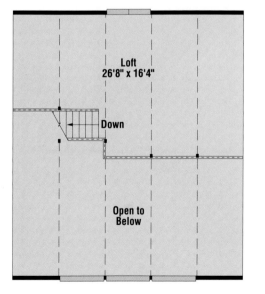

A window wall captures the view from the kitchen, living and dining rooms.

Loft
26'8" x 16'4"

Down

Open to Below

Clo

Master Bedroom
13'8" x 10'11"

Clo

Bedroom 2
10'8" x 10'11"

Closet

Bath

Linen

Up

Entry

Living
16'0" x 15'6"

Kitchen
10'8" x 6'3"

Dining
10'8" x 7'3"

Deck
Optional

Aspen

- Bedrooms: 2
- Bathrooms: 1
- Master bedroom on first floor
- Total Area: 1189 sq. ft.
- First Floor: 806 sq. ft.
- Other Floor: 383 sq. ft.
- Size: 28' x 30'
- Entry: Side
- Photos of Chalets on pages 48–49.

Chalet

Stowe

- Bedrooms: 2
- Bathrooms: 2
- Master bedroom on second floor
- Total Area: 1294 sq. ft.
- First Floor: 833 sq. ft.
- Other Floor: 461 sq. ft.
- Size: 25' x 36'
- Entry: Front
- Photos of Chalets on pages 48–49.

Tahoe

- Bedrooms: 3
- Bathrooms: 2
- Master bedroom on second floor
- Total Area: 1596 sq. ft.
- First Floor: 1041 sq. ft.
- Other Floor: 555 sq. ft.
- Size: 27' x 40'
- Entry: Side
- Photos of Chalets on pages 48–49.

First Floor

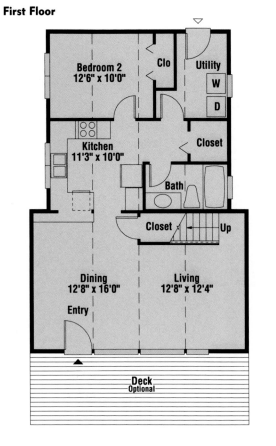

Second Floor

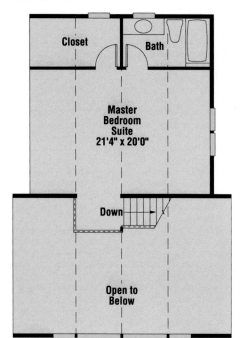

First Floor

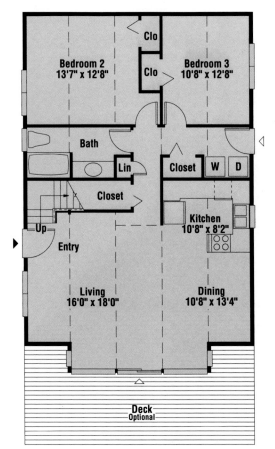

Second Floor

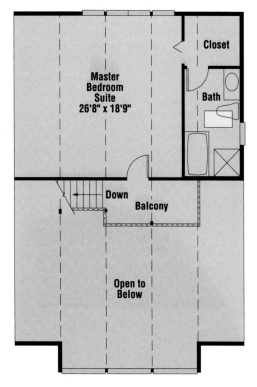

In this detail, the architectural grade glue-laminated beam meets drywall on both the side wall and ceiling.

Master Bedroom Suite
21'4" x 17'4"

Bath

Walk-In Closet

Down

Open to Below

Bedroom 2
10'8" x 13'5"

Bath

Kitchen
7'2" x 11'5"

Closet

Up

Closet

Entry

Dining
10'8" x 15'4"

Living
10'8" x 15'4"

Deck
Optional

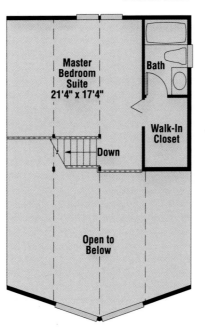

This detail shows the glue-laminated beam meeting dry-wall on the side wall and wood ceiling liner above.

Prow

Coronado

- Bedrooms: 2
- Bathrooms: 2
- Master bedroom on second floor
- Total Area: 1020 sq. ft.
- First Floor: 689 sq. ft.
- Other Floor: 331 sq. ft.
- Size: 21' x 34'
- Entry: Side
- Photos of Prows on pages 50–55.

Chesapeake

- Bedrooms: 3
- Bathrooms: 2
- Master bedroom on second floor
- Total Area: 1888 sq. ft.
- First Floor: 1093 sq. ft.
- Other Floor: 795 sq. ft.
- Size: 29' x 42'
- Entry: Side
- Photos of Prows on pages 50–55.

Second Floor

First Floor

Balcony

Master Bedroom Suite
26'8" x 12'0"

Down

Bath

Dressing

Closet

Open to Below

Office
16'0" x 20'0"

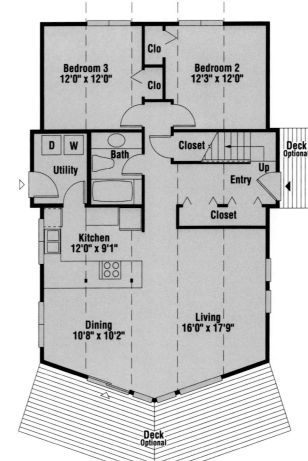

Bedroom 3
12'0" x 12'0"

Clo

Bedroom 2
12'3" x 12'0"

Clo

D **W**

Closet

Bath

Utility

Entry

Up

Deck
Optional

Closet

Kitchen
12'0" x 9'1"

Dining
10'8" x 10'2"

Living
16'0" x 17'9"

Deck
Optional

Prow

Catalina

- Bedrooms: 2
- Bathrooms: 1
- Master bedroom on first floor
- Total Area: 1252 sq. ft.
- First Floor: 790 sq. ft.
- Other Floor: 462 sq. ft.
- Size: 21' x 39'
- Entry: Side
- Photos of Prows on pages 50–55.

Greenbriar

- Bedrooms: 3
- Bathrooms: 2
- Master bedroom on second floor
- Total Area: 1626 sq. ft.
- First Floor: 1019 sq. ft.
- Other Floor: 607 sq. ft.
- Size: 27' x 40'
- Entry: Side
- Photos of Prows on pages 50–55.

First Floor

Master Bedroom 10'8" x 14'2"

Bedroom 2 10'8" x 10'1"

Closet

W/D Closet

Bath

Lin

Closet

Kitchen 7'5" x 8'10"

Up

Entry

Living 10'8" x 13'11"

Dining 10'8" x 11'5"

Deck Optional

Second Floor

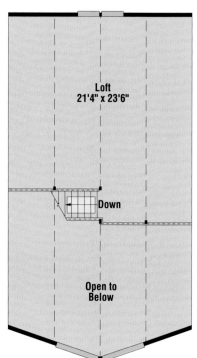

Loft 21'4" x 23'6"

Down

Open to Below

In this detail, the glue-laminated beam meets wood on both the side wall and ceiling.

First Floor

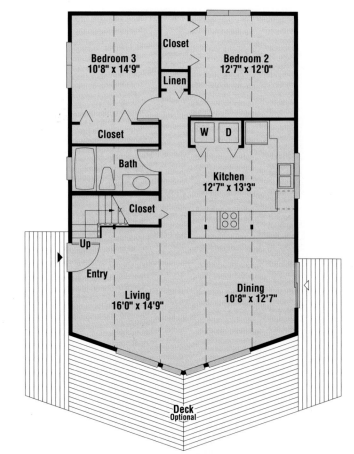

Bedroom 3 10'8" x 14'9"

Closet

Bedroom 2 12'7" x 12'0"

Linen

Closet

W D

Bath

Kitchen 12'7" x 13'3"

Closet

Up

Entry

Living 16'0" x 14'9"

Dining 10'8" x 12'7"

Deck Optional

Second Floor

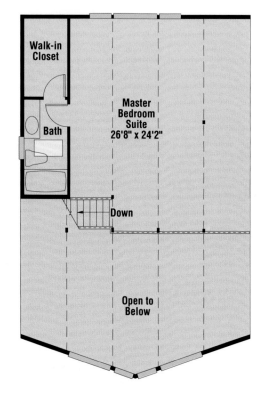

Walk-in Closet

Bath

Master Bedroom Suite 26'8" x 24'2"

Down

Open to Below

In this Alaska Greenbriar, the owners chose a Polar Cap II roof and deleted some upper windows in the prow.

This customized
Capistrano is located
in Tahoe.

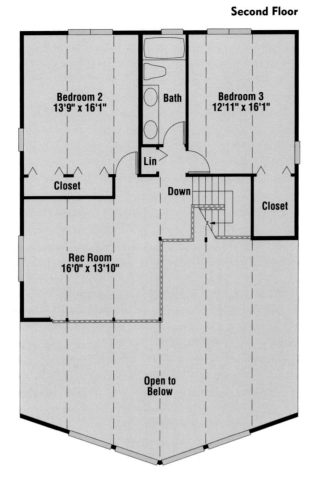

Bedroom 2
13'9" x 16'1"

Bath

Bedroom 3
12'11" x 16'1"

Closet

Lin

Down

Closet

Rec Room
16'0" x 13'10"

Open to
Below

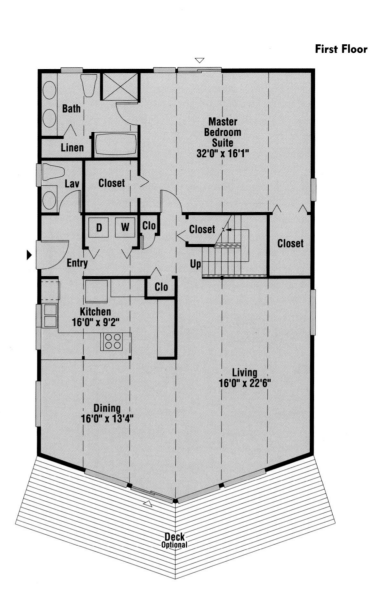

Bath

Master
Bedroom
Suite
32'0" x 16'1"

Linen

Lav

Closet

D   W   Clo

Closet

Closet

Entry

Up

Clo

Kitchen
16'0" x 9'2"

Living
16'0" x 22'6"

Dining
16'0" x 13'4"

Deck
Optional

Prow

Capistrano

- Bedrooms: 3
- Bathrooms: 2 Full & 1 Half
- Master bedroom on first floor
- Total Area: 2305 sq. ft.
- First Floor: 1461 sq. ft.
- Other Floor: 844 sq. ft.
- Size: 32' x 48'
- Entry: Side
- Photos of Prows on pages 50–55.

Niagara

- Bedrooms: 1
- Bathrooms: 1
- Master bedroom on first floor
- Total Area: 768 sq. ft.
- First Floor: 507 sq. ft.
- Other Floor: 261 sq. ft.
- Size: 21' x 26'
- Entry: Side
- Photos of Prows on pages 50–55.

This detail shows the
2x2 rails and 2x4 top
rail in our all-cedar
deck package.

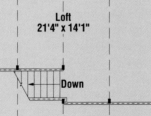

Loft
21'4" x 14'1"

Down

Open to
Below

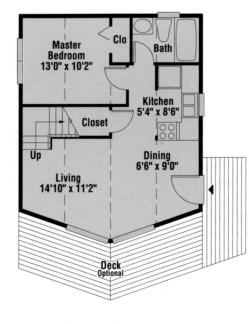

Clo

Master
Bedroom
13'0" x 10'2"

Bath

Kitchen
5'4" x 8'6"

Closet

Up

Dining
6'6" x 9'0"

Living
14'10" x 11'2"

Deck
Optional

Master bedroom
retreat upstairs with
fabulous view.

Prow

Haliburton

- Bedrooms: 2
- Bathrooms:
  1 Full & 1 Three-quarter
- Master bedroom on second floor
- Total Area: 2043 sq. ft.
- First Floor: 1360 sq. ft.
- Other Floor: 683 sq. ft.
- Size: 37' x 47'
- Entry: Side
- Photos of Prows on pages 50–55.

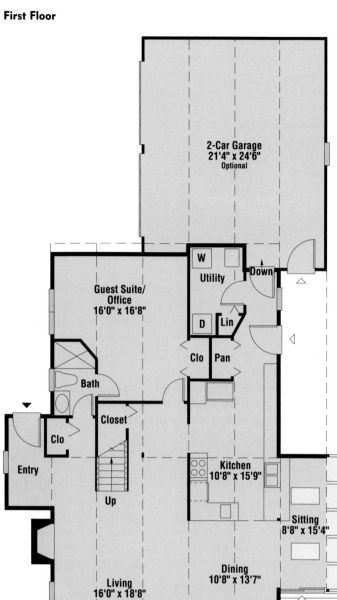

2-Car Garage
21'4" x 24'6"
Optional

W
Utility
Down

Guest Suite/Office
16'0" x 16'8"

D | Lin

Clo | Pan

Bath

Closet

Clo

Entry

Up

Kitchen
10'8" x 15'9"

Sitting
8'8" x 15'4"

Skywall - optional

Dining
10'8" x 13'7"

Living
16'0" x 18'8"

Deck
Optional

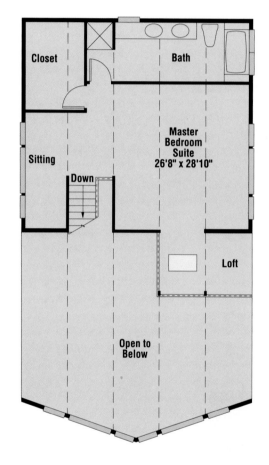

A second sink
provides another
workstation in this
colorful kitchen.

Closet

Bath

Sitting

Down

Master Bedroom Suite
26'8" x 28'10"

Open to Below

Loft

An optional skywall
rests on a 3-foot
basewall for con-
venience in placing
furniture.

Second Floor

Office/
Bedroom 2
13'4" x 13'11"

Open to
Below

Bedroom 3
13'4" x 13'11"

Closet

Closet

Bath

Lin Down

Bath

Clo

Clo

Open to
Below

Master Suite

Open to
Below

Master
Bedroom
21'4" x 13'4"

Balcony

The owners substituted a half wall for an open rail in their master bedroom.

First Floor

Deck
Optional

D

W

Family
29'4" x 13'11"

Utility
8'0" x 13'11"

Lin Closet

Clo Closet

Up

Bath

Kitchen
15'2" x 11'10"

Clo

Entry

Dining
18'8" x 13'4"

Down

Living
21'4" x 13'4"

Down

Deck
Optional

Sunroom
Optional
21'4" x 10'4"

A 7-bay sunroom off the living room is optional.

Glue-laminated beams and wood ceilings add richness to the living room.

Prow

Shenandoah

- Bedrooms: 3
- Bathrooms: 3
- Master bedroom on second floor
- Total Area: 2489 sq. ft.
- First Floor: 1467 sq. ft.
- Other Floor: 1022 sq. ft.
- Size: 39' x 42'
- Entry: Side
- Photos of Prows on pages 50–55.

By adding a second dormer to their solid cedar Teton, John and Carol gained cost-efficient square footage—and great views.

Solid cedar Lindals have such an airtight fit that no caulking is required between the timbers. And because the timbers are precut for each home and individually labeled for layer and location, construction is fast and easy.

Second Floor

Closet

Master Bedroom Suite
21'4" x 20'0"

Bath

Lin

Down

First Floor

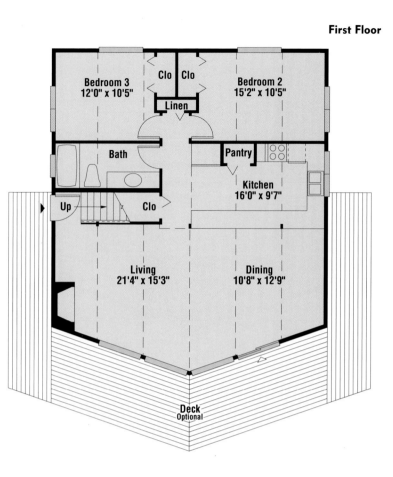

Clo | Clo

Bedroom 3
12'0" x 10'5"

Linen

Bedroom 2
15'2" x 10'5"

Bath

Pantry

Kitchen
16'0" x 9'7"

Up

Clo

Living
21'4" x 15'3"

Dining
10'8" x 12'9"

Deck
Optional

John and Carol in front of their custom Teton: "We are planning a deck in the spring."

Summit

Teton

- Bedrooms: 3
- Bathrooms: 2
- Master bedroom on second floor
- Total Area: 1482 sq. ft.
- First Floor: 1079 sq. ft.
- Other Floor: 403 sq. ft.
- Size: 32' x 36'
- Entry: Side
- Photos of Summits on pages 56–59.

"We'd been planning our dream home in the country for about four years.

Finally, we found our two acres at the top of Hockley Valley—and nine months later,

we moved into our dream home." John and Carol McDonald, ON

Summit

Whitney

- Bedrooms: 2
- Bathrooms: 2
- Master bedroom on second floor
- Total Area: 1223 sq. ft.
- First Floor: 917 sq. ft.
- Other Floor: 306 sq. ft.
- Size: 32' x 31'
  Entry: Side
- Photos of Summits on pages 56–59.

Sierra

- Bedrooms: 3
- Bathrooms: 2
- Master bedroom on second floor
- Total Area: 1228 sq. ft.
- First Floor: 912 sq. ft.
- Other Floor: 316 sq. ft.
- Size: 27' x 37'
- Entry: Side
- Photos of Summits on pages 56–59.

First Floor

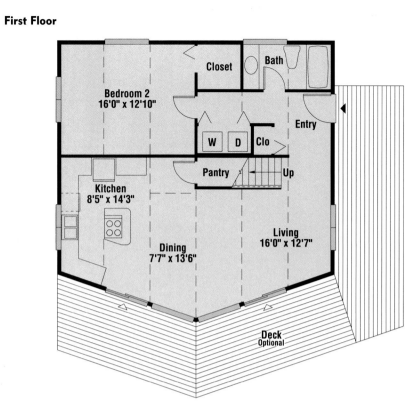

Closet

Bath

Bedroom 2
16'0" x 12'10"

Entry

W   D   Clo

Pantry   Up

Kitchen
8'5" x 14'3"

Living
16'0" x 12'7"

Dining
7'7" x 13'6"

Deck
Optional

Second Floor

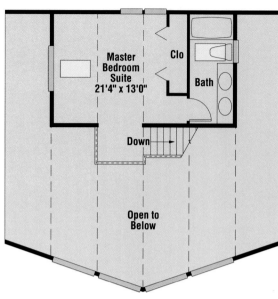

Master Bedroom Suite
21'4" x 13'0"

Clo

Bath

Down

Open to Below

The owners opted for their own window and door arrangement in the prow.

First Floor

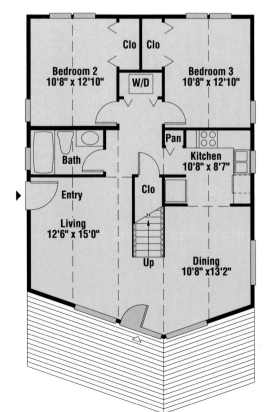

Clo   Clo

Bedroom 2
10'8" x 12'10"

W/D

Bedroom 3
10'8" x 12'10"

Bath

Pan

Kitchen
10'8" x 8'7"

Entry

Clo

Living
12'6" x 15'0"

Up

Dining
10'8" x13'2"

Second Floor

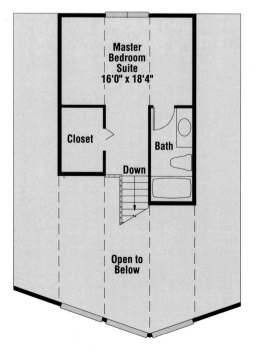

Master Bedroom Suite
16'0" x 18'4"

Closet

Bath

Down

Open to Below

In high wind, snow or earthquake areas, some codes require mechanical connections between post and beam.

**Master
Bedroom
Suite**
21'4" x 16'0"

Bath

Closet

Down

D
W

Entry

Bath

Bedroom 2
16'0" x 15'10"

Closet

Kitchen
10'8" x 10'5"

Closet

Closet

Closet

Living
16'0" x 16'5"

Up

Dining
12'5" x 18'0"

Deck
Optional

This detail shows the
opening adjustable
tension scissors hard-
ware in an awning
window.

This detail shows the
champagne-colored
rotogear crank handle
on the window.

Summit

Shasta

- Bedrooms: 2
- Bathrooms: 2
- Master bedroom on second floor
- Total Area: 1494 sq. ft.
- First Floor: 1109 sq. ft.
- Other Floor: 385 sq. ft.
- Size: 32' x 37'
- Entry: Back
- Photos of Summits on
  pages 56–59.

Second Floor

First Floor

**Master
Bedroom
Suite**
21'4" x 17'0"

Bath

Closet

Down

Clo

Bath

Entry

Clo

Bedroom 3
10'5" x 13'4"

W **D**

Lin

Bedroom 2
13'7" x 16'11"

Lin

Up

Closet

Closet

Living
21'4" x 14'7"

Dining
10'8" x 16'5"

Kitchen
10'8" x 12'11"

Deck
Optional

Olympic

- Bedrooms: 3
- Bathrooms: 2
- Master bedroom on second floor
- Total Area: 1690 sq. ft.
- First Floor: 1346 sq. ft.
- Other Floor: 344 sq. ft.
- Size: 43' x 35'
- Entry: Back
- Photos of Summits on
  pages 56–59.

View

Malibu

- Bedrooms: 2
- Bathroom: 1
- Total Area: 907 sq. ft.
- Size: 27' x 34'
- Entry: Side
- Photos of Views on pages 60–61.

Riviera

- Bedrooms: 3
- Bathrooms: 2
- Total Area: 1093 sq. ft.
- Size: 29' x 41'
- Entry: Side
- Photos of Views on pages 60–61.

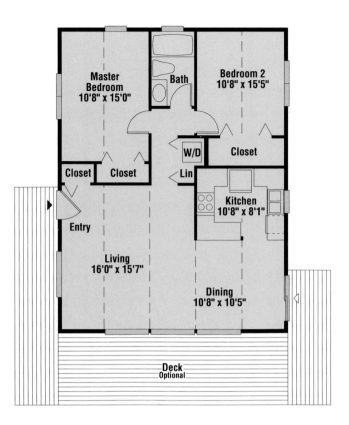

Master Bedroom 10'8" x 15'0"

Bath

Bedroom 2 10'8" x 15'5"

Closet

W/D

Closet

Lin

Closet   Closet

Kitchen 10'8" x 8'1"

Entry

Living 16'0" x 15'7"

Dining 10'8" x 10'5"

Deck
Optional

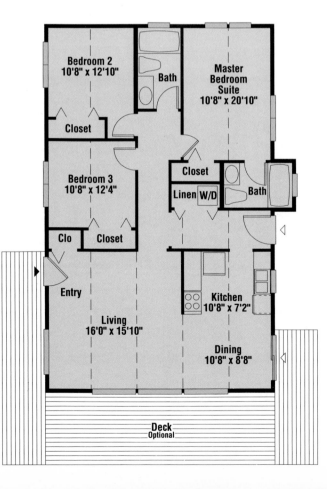

Bedroom 2 10'8" x 12'10"

Bath

Master Bedroom Suite 10'8" x 20'10"

Closet

Bedroom 3 10'8" x 12'4"

Closet

Linen W/D

Bath

Clo   Closet

Entry

Kitchen 10'8" x 7'2"

Living 16'0" x 15'10"

Dining 10'8" x 8'8"

Deck
Optional

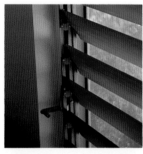

Wood and glass louvered windows are popular in tropical climates.

Capri I

Master Bedroom
10'8" x 12'4"

Bath

Bedroom 2
10'8" x 12'4"

Closet

W/D Clo

Closet

Entry

Kitchen/Dining
12'7" x 11'8"

Living
14'1" x 14'8"

Deck
Optional

Capri II

Bedroom 3
10'8" x 12'4"

Bath

Bedroom 2
10'8" x 12'4"

Walk-in Closet

Bath

Closet

W/D Clo

Closet

Entry

Master Bedroom Suite
13'10" x 18'0"

Closet

Kitchen/Dining
12'7" x 11'8"

Living
14'1" x 14'8"

Deck
Optional

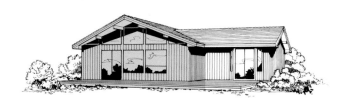

Capri III

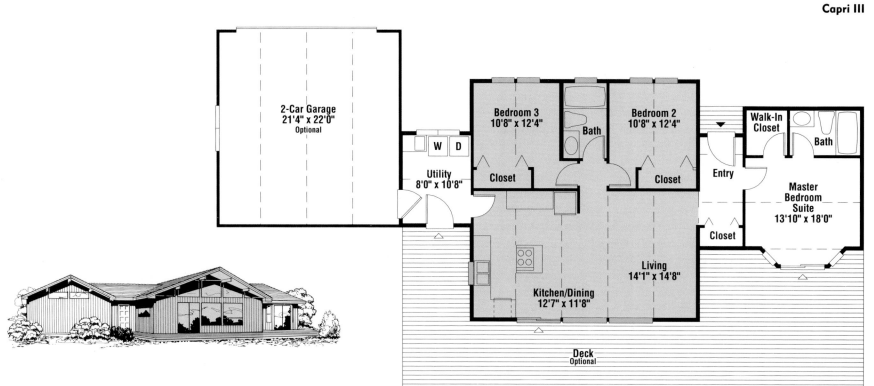

2-Car Garage
21'4" x 22'0"
Optional

W D

Utility
8'0" x 10'8"

Bedroom 3
10'8" x 12'4"

Bath

Bedroom 2
10'8" x 12'4"

Walk-In Closet

Bath

Closet

Closet

Entry

Master Bedroom Suite
13'10" x 18'0"

Closet

Kitchen/Dining
12'7" x 11'8"

Living
14'1" x 14'8"

Deck
Optional

View

Capri I

- Bedrooms: 2
- Bathrooms: 1
- Total Area: 720 sq. ft.
- Size: 27' x 27'
- Entry: Side
- Photos of Views on pages 60–61.

Capri II

- Bedrooms: 3
- Bathrooms: 2
- Total Area: 1025 sq. ft.
- Size: 46' x 27'
- Entry: Back
- Photos of Views on pages 60–61.

Capri III

- Bedrooms: 3
- Bathrooms: 2
- Total Area: 1113 sq. ft.
- Size: 54' x 27'
- Entry: Back
- Photos of Views on pages 60–61.

The Capri I, II and III illustrate "The House That Grows" concept, described on pages 138–139. As you study plans, keep this growth potential in mind.

Color shading indicates starter home (Capri I).

View

Waikiki I without Basement

- Bedrooms: 2
- Bathrooms:
  1 Full & 1 Three-quarter
- Total Area: 1184 sq. ft.
- Size: 32' x 37'
- Entry: Side
- Photos of Views on pages 60–61.

Waikiki II with basement

- Bedrooms: 3
- Bathrooms:
  2 Full & 1 Three-quarter
- Master bedroom on first floor
- Total Area: 1744 sq. ft.
- First Floor: 1153 sq. ft.
- Other Floor: 591 sq. ft.
- Size: 32' x 37'
- Entry: Side
- Photos of Views on pages 60–61.

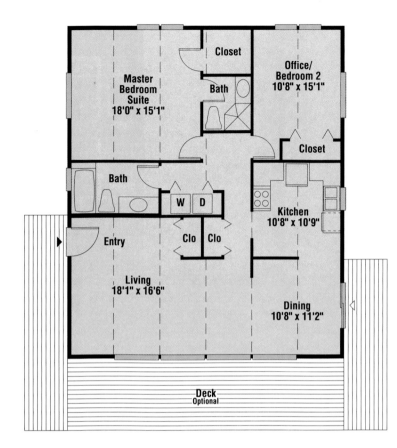

Closet

**Office/
Bedroom 2
10'8" x 15'1"**

**Master
Bedroom
Suite
18'0" x 15'1"**

Bath

Closet

Bath

W **D**

**Kitchen
10'8" x 10'9"**

Entry

Clo **Clo**

**Living
18'1" x 16'6"**

**Dining
10'8" x 11'2"**

**Deck
Optional**

The Waikiki I and II
show how easy it is
to modify a plan for
a sloped site by
building on a daylight
basement.
- Add a staircase
- Move the utilities
  downstairs
- Relocate the 2
  bathrooms on
  main floor
- Daylight basement
  allows for a third
  bedroom and
  bathroom, recre-
  ation room, full utility
  room—and lots
  of storage

First Floor

**Master
Bedroom
Suite
18'0" x 15'1"**

Closet

**Office/
Bedroom 2
10'8" x 15'1"**

Lin

Closet

Bath

Bath

Clo

**Kitchen
10'8" x 10'9"**

Entry

Down

**Living
18'1" x 16'6"**

**Dining
10'8" x 11'2"**

**Deck
Optional**

Daylight Basement

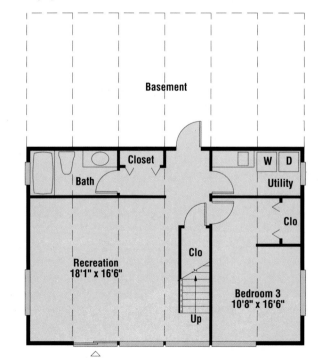

Basement

Bath

Closet

W **D**

Utility

Clo

**Recreation
18'1" x 16'6"**

Clo

Up

**Bedroom 3
10'8" x 16'6"**

Top Knot

Master Bedroom
Suite
16'0" x 16'3"

Bath

Clo

Down

First Floor

Bedroom 2
10'8" x 12'5"

Clo

Entry

Bath

Bedroom 3
10'8" x 12'5"

Clo

Clo

Up

Clo

Lin | W | D

Closet

Kitchen
9'5" x 10'8"

Living
16'0" x 14'4"

Dining
11'11" x 10'10"

Deck
Optional

Panorama

Acapulco

- Bedrooms: 3
- Bathrooms: 2
- Master bedroom on second floor
- Total Area: 1226 sq. ft.
- First Floor: 999 sq. ft.
- Other Floor: 227 sq. ft.
- Size: 37' x 26'
- Entry: Back
- Photos of Panoramas on pages 62–63.

Monaco I with loft

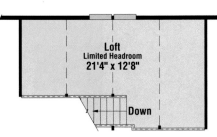

Loft
Limited Headroom
21'4" x 12'8"

Down

Monaco II with Top Knot

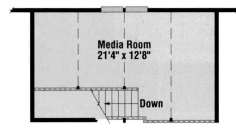

Media Room
21'4" x 12'8"

Down

First Floor

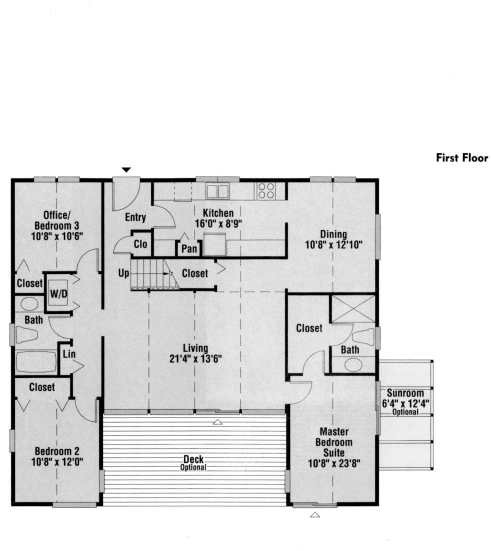

Office/
Bedroom 3
10'8" x 10'6"

Entry

Kitchen
16'0" x 8'9"

Dining
10'8" x 12'10"

Clo

Pan

Closet

W/D

Up

Closet

Bath

Closet

Lin

Living
21'4" x 13'6"

Bath

Closet

Bedroom 2
10'8" x 12'0"

Deck
Optional

Master
Bedroom
Suite
10'8" x 23'8"

Sunroom
6'4" x 12'4"
Optional

Monaco I & II

- Bedrooms: 3
- Bathrooms:
  1 Full & 1 Three-quarter
- Master bedroom on first floor
- Total Area: 1564 sq. ft.
- First Floor: 1337 sq. ft.
- Monaco I Loft: 227 sq. ft.
  (low headroom)
- Monaco II Topknot: 227 sq. ft.
- Size: 43' x 37'
- Entry: Back
- Photos of Panoramas on pages 62–63.

Monaco II with topknot

Gambrel

Concord

- Bedrooms: 3
- Bathrooms: 2
- Master bedroom on second floor
- Total Area: 1295 sq. ft.
- First Floor: 667 sq. ft.
- Other Floor: 628 sq. ft.
- Size: 21' x 31'
- Entry: Side
- Photos of Gambrels on page 65.

Lexington

- Bedrooms: 3
- Bathrooms: 1 Full & 1 Half
- Master bedroom on second floor
- Total Area: 1615 sq. ft.
- First Floor: 827 sq. ft.
- Other Floor: 788 sq. ft.
- Size: 27' x 31'
- Entry: Side
- Photos of Gambrels on page 65.

First Floor

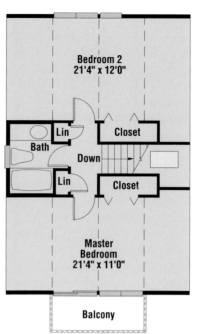

Lin

Clo

Bath

Bedroom 3
10'8" x 14'4"

W/D

Closet

Kitchen
10'8" x 8'7"

Up

Entry

Dining
10'8" x 8'5"

Living
10'8" x 13'4"

Deck
Optional

Second Floor

Bedroom 2
21'4" x 12'0"

Lin

Closet

Bath

Down

Lin

Closet

Up

Master
Bedroom
21'4" x 11'0"

Balcony

This detail shows the
fascia, beams, soffit
and tongue and
groove cedar siding.

First Floor

D   W   Lav

Kitchen
10'8" x 11'5"

Family
16'0" x 13'9"

Closet

Up

Entry

Dining
10'8" x 13'7"

Living
16'0" x 13'7"

Deck
Optional

Second Floor

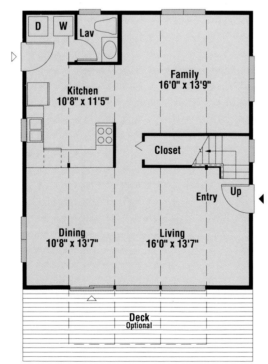

Bedroom 3
13'1" x 11'2"

Bedroom 2
13'7" x 11'2"

Closet

Closet

Bath

Down

Closet

Lin

Closet

Master
Bedroom
Suite
26'8" x 13'7"

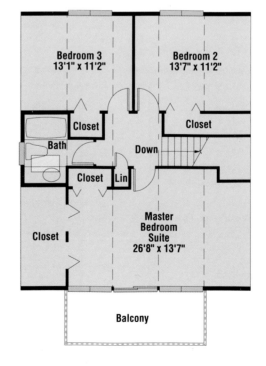

Balcony

A balcony off the
master bedroom
is included in the
Lexington.

The high ceiling
creates an airy,
open feeling in the
U-shaped kitchen.

Bedroom 3
12'8" x 10'8"

Bedroom 2
10'8" x 16'0"

Clo

Master Bedroom Suite
14'0" x 18'5"

Closet

Closet

Bath

Bath

W D

Entry

Kitchen
10'8" x 9'6"

Living
26'8" x 16'0"

Dining
10'8" x 9'5"

Deck
Optional

Deck
Optional

Pole

Kona

- Bedrooms: 3
- Bathrooms: 2
- Total Area: 1376 sq. ft.
- Size: 37' x 37'
- Entry: Side
- Photos of Poles on page 64.

Sausalito

- Bedrooms: 4
- Bathrooms: 2
- Total Area: 2304 sq. ft.
- Size: 48' x 48'
- Entry: Front
- Photos of Poles on page 64.

Deck
Optional

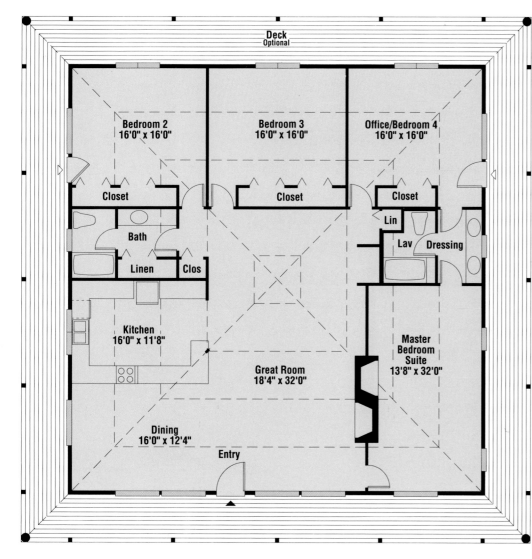

Bedroom 2
16'0" x 16'0"

Bedroom 3
16'0" x 16'0"

Office/Bedroom 4
16'0" x 16'0"

Closet

Closet

Closet

Lin

Bath

Lav

Dressing

Linen

Clos

Kitchen
16'0" x 11'8"

Great Room
18'4" x 32'0"

Master Bedroom Suite
13'8" x 32'0"

Dining
16'0" x 12'4"

Entry

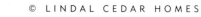

The corner bedroom
is bright and airy with
windows on 2 walls.

Contempo
Prow Star

BaySide

- Bedrooms: 3
- Bathrooms: 2
- Total Area: 1514 sq. ft.
- Size: 54' x 35'
- Entry: Front
- Photos of Contempo Prow Stars on pages 68–77.

SeaSide

- Bedrooms: 2
- Bathrooms: 2
- Total Area: 1553 sq. ft.
- Size: 59' x 32'
- Entry: Back
- Photos of Contempo Prow Stars on pages 68–77.

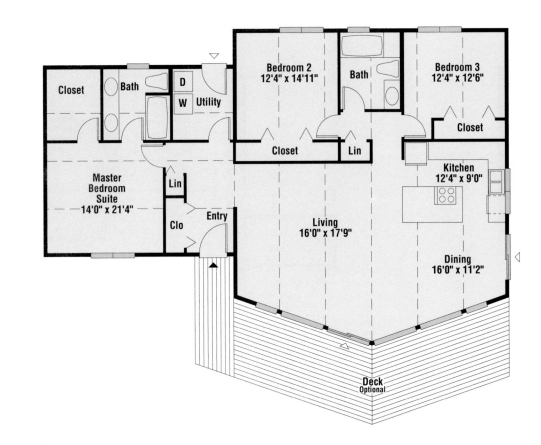

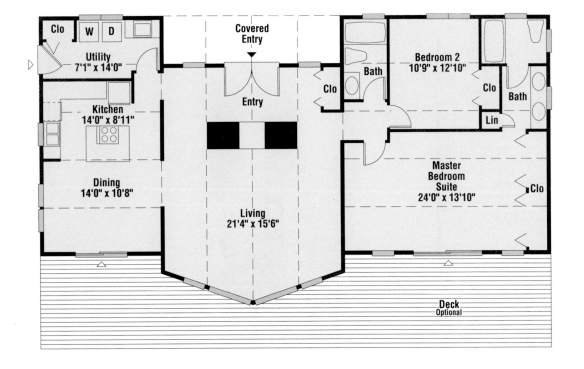

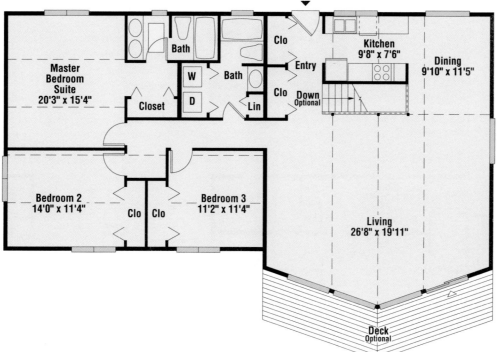

Master Bedroom Suite 20'3" x 15'4"

Bath

Clo

Kitchen 9'8" x 7'6"

Dining 9'10" x 11'5"

Entry

Bath

W D

Closet

Lin

Down Optional

Bedroom 2 14'0" x 11'4"

Clo **Clo**

Bedroom 3 11'2" x 11'4"

Living 26'8" x 19'11"

Deck Optional

Contempo Prow Star

LakeSide

- Bedrooms: 3
- Bathrooms: 2
- Total Area: 1624 sq. ft.
- Size: 57' x 33'
- Entry: Back
- Photos of Contempo Prow Stars on pages 68–77.

CapeSide

- Bedrooms: 3
- Bathrooms: 2
- Total Area: 1758 sq. ft.
- Size: 73' x 39'
- Entry: Front
- Photos of Contempo Prow Stars on pages 68–77.

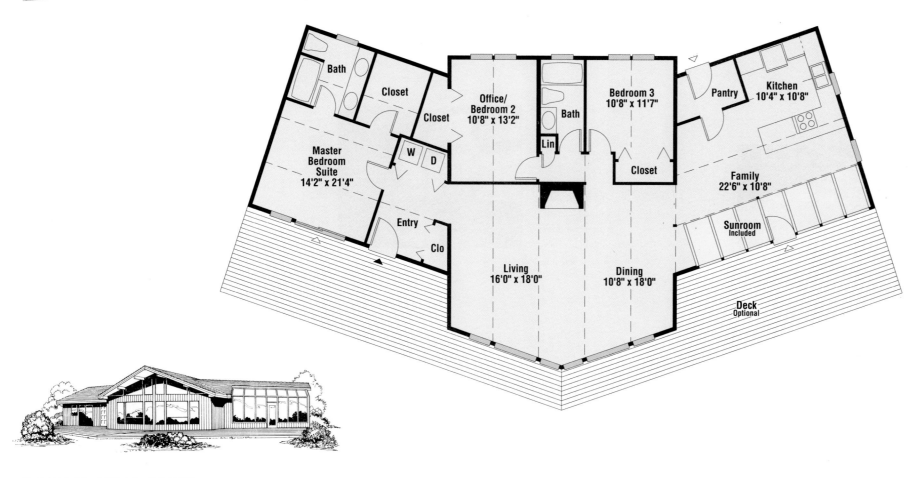

Bath

Closet

Closet

Office/ Bedroom 2 10'8" x 13'2"

Bath

Bedroom 3 10'8" x 11'7"

Pantry

Kitchen 10'4" x 10'8"

Master Bedroom Suite 14'2" x 21'4"

W D

Lin

Closet

Family 22'6" x 10'8"

Entry

Clo

Living 16'0" x 18'0"

Dining 10'8" x 18'0"

Sunroom Included

Deck Optional

Contempo
Prow Star

ParkSide

- Bedrooms: 2
- Bathrooms:
  1 Full & 1 Three-quarter
- Total Area: 1833 sq. ft.
- Size: 67' x 41'
- Entry: Back
- Photos of Contempo Prow Stars
  on pages 68–77.

The ParkSide is the
home chronicled in
Deer Parks Journal
on pages 6, 9, 16,
74–77 and 263.

Note the connection
of the beams over the
kitchen—functional
and aesthetically
pleasing, too.

2-Car Garage
21'4" x 22'0"
Optional

Utility
16'11" x 6'7"

Clo

Bath

Lin

**Walk-in
Closet**

Bath

Clo

Lin

Down

Down
Optional

Entry

Kitchen
17'6" x 13'4"

Closet

Bedroom 2
12'0" x 14'0"

Living
21'4" x 24'0"

**Master
Bedroom
Suite**
16'0" x 24'0"

Down

Deck
Optional

Dining
17'6" x 13'8"

Sunroom
Included

A hip sunroom
(included) wraps
around the dining
room.

The owners sub-
stituted custom
curved windows
in the prow front.

190

The owners opted for cedar ceiling liner.

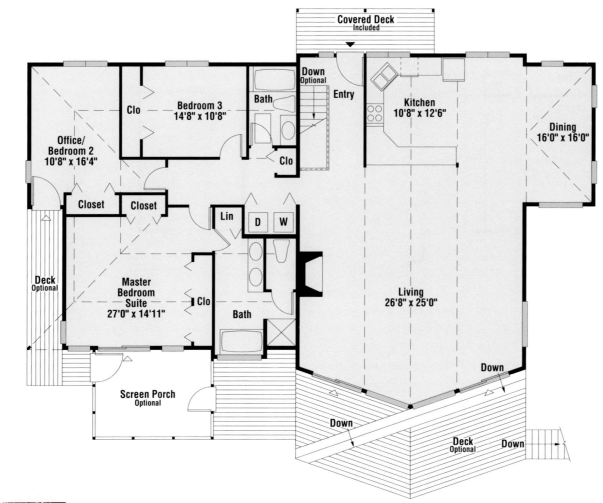

Covered Deck
Included

Down
Optional

Entry

Kitchen
10'8" x 12'6"

Dining
16'0" x 16'0"

Bath

Clo

Bedroom 3
14'8" x 10'8"

Clo

Office/
Bedroom 2
10'8" x 16'4"

Closet

Closet

Lin

D **W**

Deck
Optional

Master
Bedroom
Suite
27'0" x 14'11"

Clo

Bath

Living
26'8" x 25'0"

Down

Screen Porch
Optional

Down

Deck
Optional

Down

A gable roof crowns
the screened porch
(optional).

Contempo Prow
Star Variations

OceanSide

- Bedrooms: 3
- Bathrooms: 2
- Total Area: 2062 sq. ft.
- Size: 66' x 40'
- Entry: Back
- Photos of Contempo Prow Star Variations on pages 68–77.

A prow window wall
in the living room
captures the
lake view.

191

Contempo Prow Star Variations

HillSide

- Bedrooms: 3
- Bathrooms: 3 Full & 1 Half
- Master bedroom on lower floor
- Total Area: 2227 sq. ft.
- First Floor: 877 sq. ft.
- Other Floor: 1350 sq. ft.
- Size: 55' x 32'
- Entry: Back
- Photos of Contempo Prow Star Variations on pages 68–77.

In the HillSide—unlike most daylight basement homes—bedrooms are on the entry level and the main living spaces—including the kitchen—are downstairs, handy to the yard.

First Floor

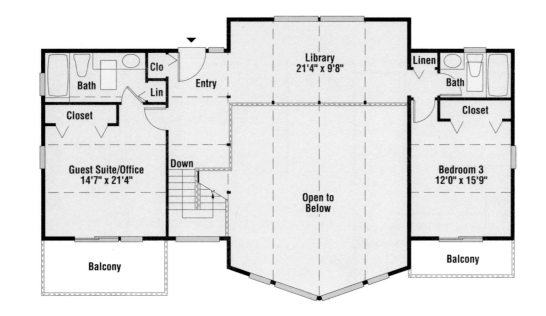

Daylight Basement

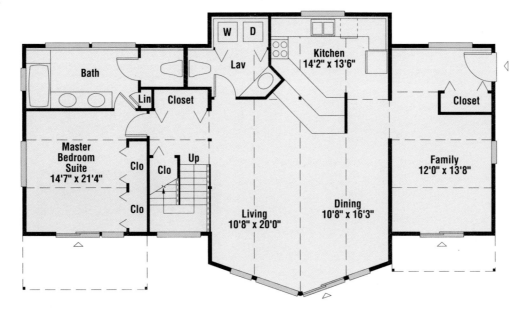

Roof Options

Cedar Frame Specification. Cavity roof system, R-33.

Cedar Frame Specification. Polar Cap cavity roof system, up to R-63. Optional.

Solid Cedar Specification. Rigid Insulation roof system, R-38.

Prow window wall
frames the view.
These owners pre-
ferred to delete the
sliding glass doors.

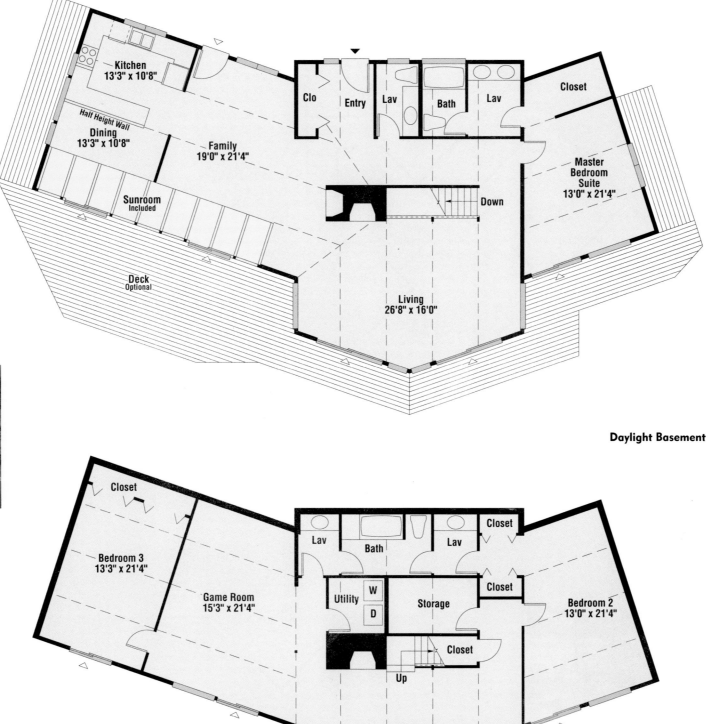

Kitchen
13'3" x 10'8"

Clo **Entry** **Lav** **Bath** **Lav** **Closet**

Half Height Wall
Dining
13'3" x 10'8"

Family
19'0" x 21'4"

**Master
Bedroom
Suite**
13'0" x 21'4"

Sunroom
Included

Down

Deck
Optional

Living
26'8" x 16'0"

Contempo Prow
Star Variations

CliffSide

- Bedrooms: 3
- Bathrooms: 2 Full & 1 Half
- Master bedroom on first floor
- Total Area: 3480 sq. ft.
- First Floor: 1723 sq. ft.
- Other Floor: 1757 sq. ft.
- Size: 73' x 41'
- Entry: Back
- Photos of Contempo Prow Star Variations on pages 68–77.

A 9-bay sunroom
is included in the
CliffSide. Again,
these owners elimi-
nated the sliding
glass doors.

Daylight Basement

Closet

Bedroom 3
13'3" x 21'4"

Lav **Bath** **Lav** **Closet**

Game Room
15'3" x 21'4"

Utility W D **Storage** **Closet**

Bedroom 2
13'0" x 21'4"

Closet

Up

Rec Room
26'8" x 16'0"

Contempo Prow Star Variations

RiverSide

- Bedrooms: 3
- Bathrooms: 2
- Master bedroom on first floor
- Total Area: 2295 sq. ft.
- First Floor: 1927 sq. ft.
- Other Floor: 368 sq. ft.
- Size: 64' x 54'
- Entry: Side
- Photos of Contempo Prow Star Variations on pages 68–77.

First Floor

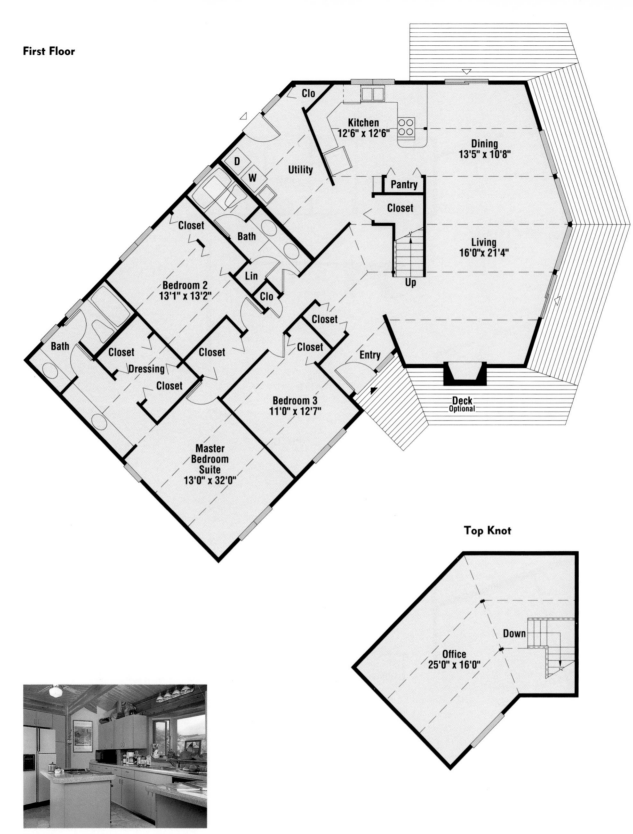

Clo

Kitchen
12'6" x 12'6"

Dining
13'5" x 10'8"

D

W

Utility

Pantry

Closet

Closet

Living
16'0"x 21'4"

Bath

Up

Bedroom 2
13'1" x 13'2"

Lin

Clo

Closet

Closet

Bath

Closet

Dressing

Closet

Closet

Entry

Closet

Bedroom 3
11'0" x 12'7"

Master
Bedroom
Suite
13'0" x 32'0"

Deck
Optional

Top Knot

Down

Office
25'0" x 16'0"

Finely planed cedar
timbers invite a
wide variety of
decorating styles.

A wood framed slid-
ing glass door leads
to the deck from the
living room with its
prow front of glass.

The owners added a
bay window and an
island to their kitchen.

A three bay sunroom
(included) makes a
grand entrance.

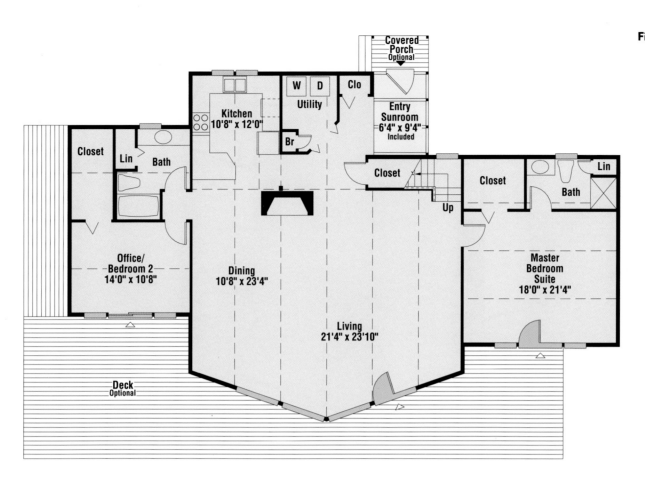

Covered
Porch
Optional

W | D | Clo
Utility

Kitchen
10'8" x 12'0"

Br

Entry
Sunroom
6'4" x 9'4"
Included

Closet

Lin

Bath

Closet

Up

Closet

Lin

Bath

Office/
Bedroom 2
14'0" x 10'8"

Dining
10'8" x 23'4"

Master
Bedroom
Suite
18'0" x 21'4"

Living
21'4" x 23'10"

Deck
Optional

Contempo Prow
Star Building Up

ValleySide

- Bedrooms: 2
- Bathrooms:
  1 Full & 1 Three-quarter
- Master bedroom on first floor
- Total Area: 1984 sq. ft.
- First Floor: 1805 sq. ft.
- Other Floor: 179 sq. ft.
- Size: 64' x 39'
- Entry: Back
- Photos of Contempo Prow Star
  Building Up on pages 78–79.

An open loft above
the living room is ideal
for a media room.

Two-story window
wall with 4/12 pitched
ceiling above.

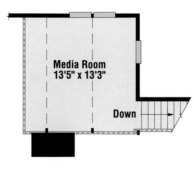

Media Room
13'5" x 13'3"

Down

Stairs with open rail
and optional open
treads lead from the
living room to the loft.

Contempo Prow
Star Building Up

CountrySide

- Bedrooms: 4
- Bathrooms: 3 Full & 1 Half
- Master bedroom on second floor
- Total Area: 3183 sq. ft.
- First Floor: 1842 sq. ft.
- Other Floor: 1341 sq. ft.
- Size: 69' x 44'
- Entry: Back
- Photos of Contempo Prow Star
  Building Up on pages 78–79.

First Floor

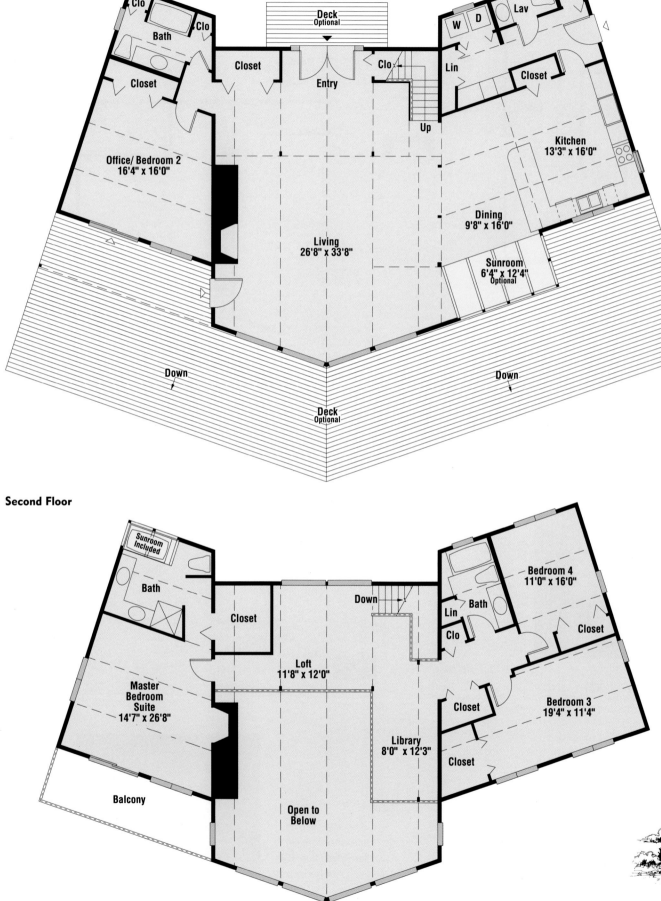

Second Floor

A peninsula forms a
convenient eating bar
between kitchen and
dining room.

A corner 2-bay skywall
with glass endwall,
topping the tub in
the master bath,
is included.

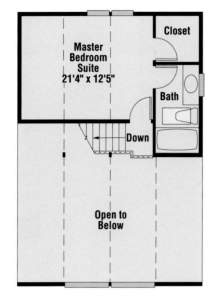

Second Floor labels:

Closet

Master
Bedroom
Suite
21'4" x 12'5"

Bath

Down

Open to
Below

First Floor labels:

Deck
Optional

Family
10'8" x 12'5"

Kitchen
10'8" x 12'5"

D

W

Clo

Bath

Linen

Bedroom 2
15'4" x 10'8"

Pantry

Up

Closet

Entry

Clo

Clo

Bedroom 3
15'4" x 10'8"

Living
21'4" x 14'9"

Deck
Optional

Chalet Star

RoseHill

- Bedrooms: 3
- Bathrooms: 2
- Master bedroom on second floor
- Total Area: 1460 sq. ft.
- First Floor: 1163 sq. ft.
- Other Floor: 297 sq. ft.
- Size: 45' x 31'
- Entry: Front
- Photos of Chalet Stars on pages 80–83.

Open 2x2 cedar rail
for balusters. Cedar
2x4 top rail. Closed
risers. A partition
below is required.

Open risers. Open
underneath.

Glue-laminated
stringers and treads
with open risers.
Open underneath.

Chalet Star

FernHill

- Bedrooms: 2
- Bathrooms: 2
- Master bedroom on second floor
- Total Area: 1499 sq. ft.
- First Floor: 1104 sq. ft.
- Other Floor: 395 sq. ft.
- Size: 40' x 31'
- Entry: Front
- Photos of Chalet Stars on pages 80–83.

First Floor

Bedroom 2
14'7" x 12'4"

Bath

Kitchen
13'2" x 11'1"

Down

2-Car Garage
22'6" x 21'4"
Optional

W   D

Closet   Lin

Dining
13'0" x 10'3"

Up

Living
21'4" x 15'0"

Entry

Deck
Optional

Closet

Second Floor

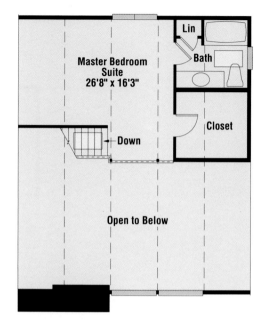

Lin

Master Bedroom
Suite
26'8" x 16'3"

Bath

Closet

Down

Open to Below

In chalets the cathedral ceiling stretches skyward.

Steel entry doors are for the truly energy conscious, but raised panel wood doors are an attractive option.

For a more open feeling, the homeowners replaced the wall between the kitchen and dining room with suspended cabinets.

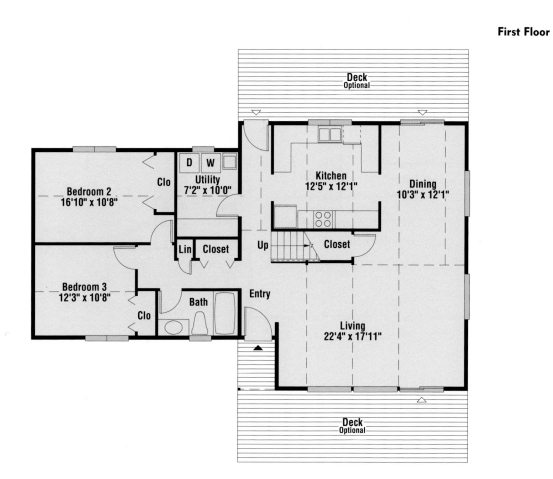

Deck
Optional

Bedroom 2
16'10" x 10'8"

Clo

D W

Utility
7'2" x 10'0"

Kitchen
12'5" x 12'1"

Dining
10'3" x 12'1"

Lin Closet

Closet

Up

Bedroom 3
12'3" x 10'8"

Clo

Bath

Entry

Living
22'4" x 17'11"

Deck
Optional

The owners eliminated the sliding glass door and moved the window in the dining room for more wall space.

Second Floor

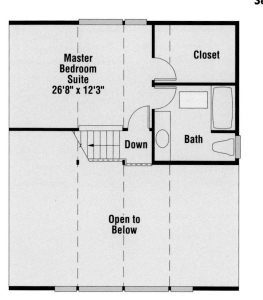

Master Bedroom Suite
26'8" x 12'3"

Closet

Down

Bath

Open to Below

Chalet Star

GlenHill

- Bedrooms: 3
- Bathrooms: 2
- Master bedroom on second floor
- Total Area: 1665 sq. ft.
- First Floor: 1287 sq. ft.
- Other Floor: 378 sq. ft.
- Size: 51' x 30'
- Entry: Front
- Photos of Chalet Stars on pages 80–83.

Chalet Star

FairHill

- Bedrooms: 3
- Bathrooms: 2
- Master bedroom on second floor
- Total Area: 2188 sq. ft.
- First Floor: 1641 sq. ft.
- Other Floor: 547 sq. ft.
- Size: 56' x 30'
- Entry: Front
- Photos of Chalet Stars on pages 80–83.

First Floor

Dining
16'0" x 12'8"

Kitchen
12'10" x 12'1"

D
W

Lin

Bath

Clo

Utility
6'6" x 12'1"

Bedroom 2
10'8" x 16'5"

Lin

Closet

Pantry

Up

Entry

Closet

Clo

Office/
Bedroom 3
12'4" x 11'4"

Living
26'8" x 13'6"

Deck
Optional

Sunroom
12'4" x 9'4"
Optional

Second Floor

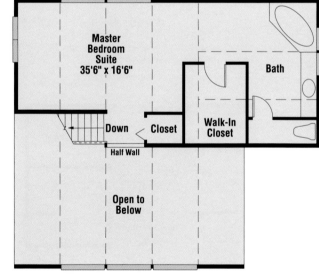

Master
Bedroom
Suite
35'6" x 16'6"

Bath

Down

Closet

Walk-In
Closet

Half Wall

Open to
Below

The 4-bay sunroom off
Bedroom 3 is optional.
Your choice.

Closeup of the
recessed front entry
and sunroom.

A compartmentalized
bathroom permits
privacy, but opens
the tub to the
bedroom.

© LINDAL CEDAR HOMES

The spacious kitchen, open to the dining room, is one feature that makes the BayVista a favorite plan.

First Floor

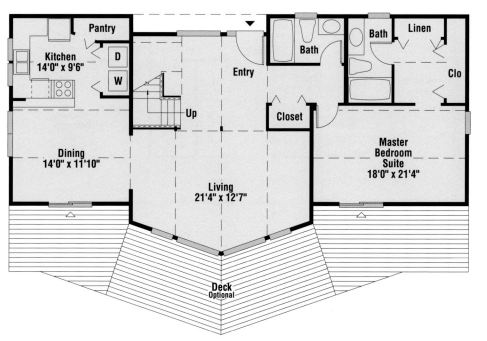

Pantry

Kitchen
14'0" x 9'6"

D
W

Bath

Bath

Linen

Clo

Entry

Up

Closet

Dining
14'0" x 11'10"

Master
Bedroom
Suite
18'0" x 21'4"

Living
21'4" x 12'7"

Deck
Optional

Second Floor

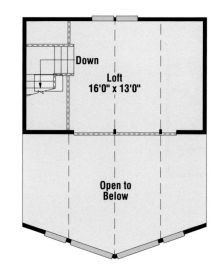

Down

Loft
16'0" x 13'0"

Open to
Below

A wood framed 3-dimensional garden window is a delightful option for over the kitchen sink.

The garden window comes with opening side panels with screens for ventilation.

Prow Star

BayVista

- Bedrooms: 1
- Bathrooms: 2
- Master bedroom on first floor
- Total Area: 1387 sq. ft.
- First Floor: 1187 sq. ft.
- Other Floor: 200 sq. ft.
- Size: 53' x 27'
- Entry: Back
- Photos of Prow Stars on pages 84–91.

Prow Star

FairVista

- Bedrooms: 2
- Bathrooms: 2 Full & 1 Half
- Master bedroom on first floor
- Total Area: 1686 sq. ft.
- First Floor: 1375 sq. ft.
- Other Floor: 311 sq. ft.
- Size: 54' x 34'
- Entry: Back
- Photos of Prow Stars on pages 84–91.

First Floor

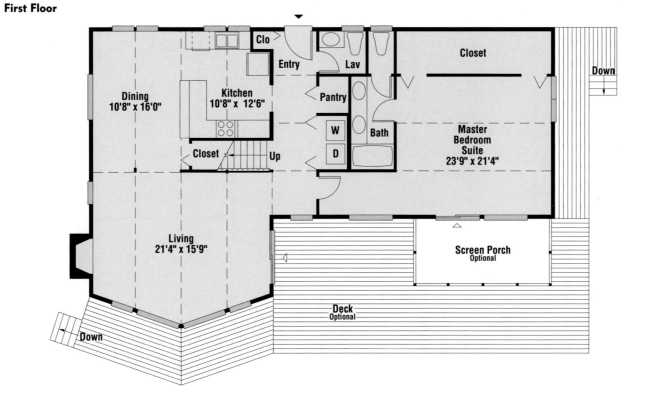

Clo
Entry
Lav
Closet
Down
Dining 10'8" x 16'0"
Kitchen 10'8" x 12'6"
Pantry
W
D
Bath
Master Bedroom Suite 23'9" x 21'4"
Closet
Up
Living 21'4" x 15'9"
Screen Porch Optional
Down
Deck Optional

Second Floor

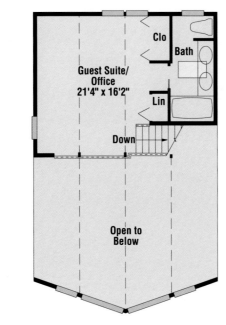

Clo
Bath
Guest Suite/ Office 21'4" x 16'2"
Lin
Down
Open to Below

These owners added
a screened porch.
Another possibility
is the new Lindal
Garden Room.
Ask your consultant
for ideas.

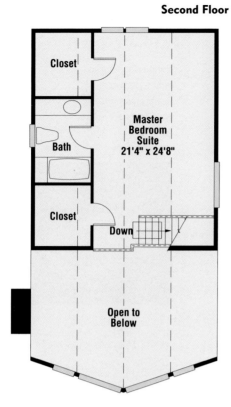

Closet

Master Bedroom Suite
21'4" x 24'8"

Bath

Closet

Down

Open to Below

Bedroom 2
10'8" x 13'11"

Bedroom 3
10'8" x 13'11"

Closet

Closet

Bath

Utility

Closet

Entry

Kitchen
14'6" x 10'8"

D W

Up

Living
21'4" x 14'4"

Dining
20'0" x 10'8"

Deck
Optional

Prow Star

SkyVista

- Bedrooms: 3
- Bathrooms: 2
- Master bedroom on second floor
- Total Area: 1744 sq. ft.
- First Floor: 1255 sq ft.
- Other Floor: 489 sq. ft.
- Size: 41' x 41'
- Entry: Back
- Photos of Prow Stars on pages 84–91.

Upstairs, dormers raise the normally sloped roof to full height outside walls—increasing usable floor space significantly.

A window wall in the prow, capturing the view, is the focal point of the living room.

chapter

PLANS
CONTEMPORARY

Prow Star

Valley Vista

- Bedrooms: 3
- Bathrooms: 2
- Master bedroom on second floor
- Total Area: 1756 sq. ft.
- First Floor: 1323 sq. ft.
- Other Floor: 433 sq. ft.
- Size: 49' x 35'
- Entry: Side
- Photos of Prow Stars on pages 84–91.

First Floor

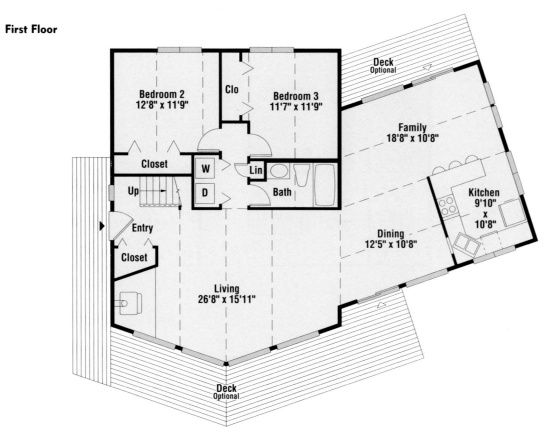

Bedroom 2
12'8" x 11'9"

Clo

Bedroom 3
11'7" x 11'9"

Deck
Optional

Family
18'8" x 10'8"

Closet

W   Lin

D   Bath

Up

Kitchen
9'10"
x
10'8"

Entry

Dining
12'5" x 10'8"

Closet

Living
26'8" x 15'11"

Deck
Optional

Second Floor

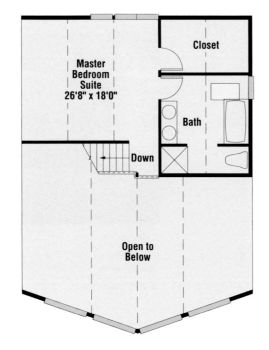

Master
Bedroom
Suite
26'8" x 18'0"

Closet

Bath

Down

Open to
Below

Put an optional sky-light (opening or fixed) anywhere you want for more natural light. Ideal in halls and stairwells.

2 ¼" cedar casing is provided for trimming doors and windows and for baseboard. Red oak is optional.

© LINDAL CEDAR HOMES

An eating bar off the island is handy for breakfast and snacks.

First Floor

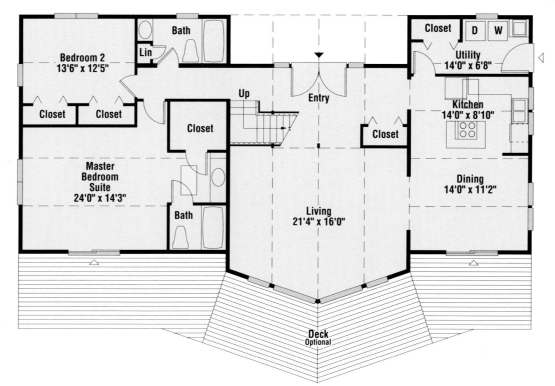

Closet

D   W

Bath

Bedroom 2
13'6" x 12'5"

Lin

Utility
14'0" x 6'8"

Up

Entry

Closet   Closet

Closet

Kitchen
14'0" x 8'10"

Master
Bedroom
Suite
24'0" x 14'3"

Closet

Bath

Living
21'4" x 16'0"

Dining
14'0" x 11'2"

Bath

Deck
Optional

Prow Star

CascadeVista

- Bedrooms: 2
- Bathrooms: 2
- Master bedroom on first floor
- Total Area: 1821 sq. ft.
- First Floor: 1551 sq. ft.
- Other Floor: 270 sq. ft.
- Size: 59' x 32'
- Entry: Back
- Photos of Prow Stars on pages 84–91.

A sunken living room and extra windows in the foyer helped personalize this home.

Second Floor

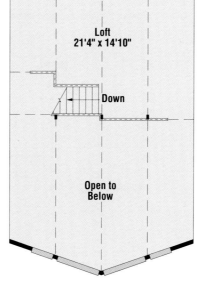

Loft
21'4" x 14'10"

Down

Open to
Below

The windows of the prow frame the view, and the deck configuration matches the prow.

Prow Star

SeaVista

- Bedrooms: 3
- Bathrooms: 2
- Master bedroom on second floor
- Total Area: 1838 sq. ft.
- First Floor: 1454 sq. ft.
- Other Floor: 384 sq. ft.
- Size: 60' x 36'
- Entry: Back
- Photos of Prow Stars on pages 84–91.

First Floor

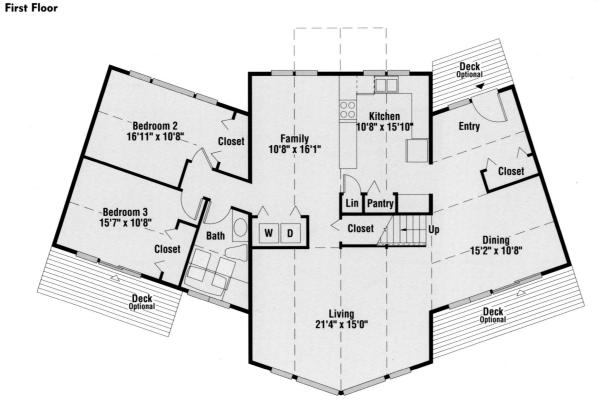

Bedroom 2
16'11" x 10'8"

Closet

Kitchen
10'8" x 15'10"

Family
10'8" x 16'1"

Entry

Closet

Bedroom 3
15'7" x 10'8"

Lin Pantry

Closet

Bath

Closet

W D

Up

Dining
15'2" x 10'8"

Deck
Optional

Living
21'4" x 15'0"

Deck
Optional

Deck
Optional

Second Floor

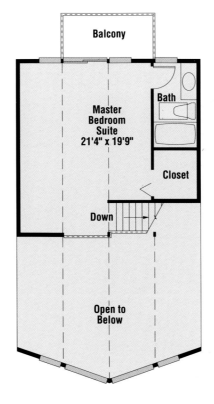

Balcony

Master
Bedroom
Suite
21'4" x 19'9"

Bath

Closet

Down

Open to
Below

The whole second floor is devoted to a master bedroom suite.

The kitchen is open to the family room— a popular feature.

Add windows and doors anywhere you like. These home-owners did in the dining room.

The architectural grade glue-laminated beams and wood trim add a luxurious note to the living room.

These owners
added cedar liner
throughout most
of their home.

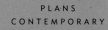

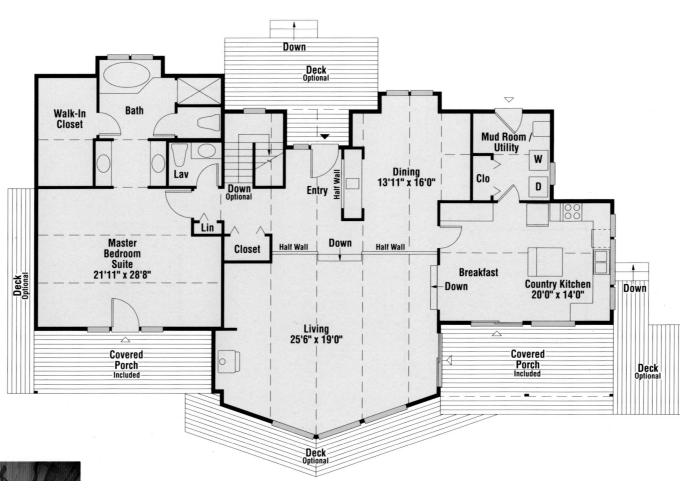

Down

Deck
Optional

**Walk-In
Closet**

Bath

**Mud Room /
Utility**

W

Lav

Clo

D

Down
Optional

Entry

Half Wall

Dining
13'11" x 16'0"

Lin

Closet

Half Wall

Down

Half Wall

**Master
Bedroom
Suite**
21'11" x 28'8"

Breakfast

Down

Country Kitchen
20'0" x 14'0"

Down

Deck Optional

Living
25'6" x 19'0"

**Covered
Porch**
Included

**Covered
Porch**
Included

Deck
Optional

Deck
Optional

Prow Star

ViewVista

- Bedrooms: 1
- Bathrooms: 1 Full & 1 Half
- Total Area: 1920 sq. ft.
- Size: 67' x 43'
- Entry: Back
- Photos of Prow Stars on
  pages 84–91.

A cedar-lined
cathedral ceiling
gives the formal entry
an elegant feeling.

Capture your view
with a prow of glass.

Astral glass, windows
and a sliding glass
door make this coun-
try kitchen a pleasure
to work in.

Prow Star

Lake Vista

- Bedrooms: 2
- Bathrooms:
  1 Full & 1 Three-quarter
- Master bedroom on second floor
- Total Area: 2017 sq. ft.
- First Floor: 1457 sq. ft.
- Other Floor: 560 sq. ft.
- Size: 47' x 37'
- Entry: Back
- Photos of Prow Stars on
  pages 84–91.

First Floor

Bedroom 2
10'8" x 17'0"

Bath

Clo

Lin

Entry

Deck Optional

Deck Optional

Kitchen
19'2" x 9'2"

D

W

Closet

Closet

Half High Wall

Up

Closet

Sitting
9'10" x 12'2"

Dining
16'2" x 19'8"

Living
21'4" x 14'5"

Deck Optional

Second Floor

Balcony

Master
Bedroom
Suite
31'4" x 17'2"

Closet

Bath

Down

Open to
Below

The country decor is a
perfect complement to
this solid cedar home.

Solid cedar timbers
add warmth to the liv-
ing room, and require
little maintenance.

Large windows pro-
vide ample natural
light in this walk-out
daylight basement.

The four-poster is
centered under an
optional skylight for
stargazing.

In the dining room, a mirrored back wall enlarges the room visually. The owners deleted the door to the garage.

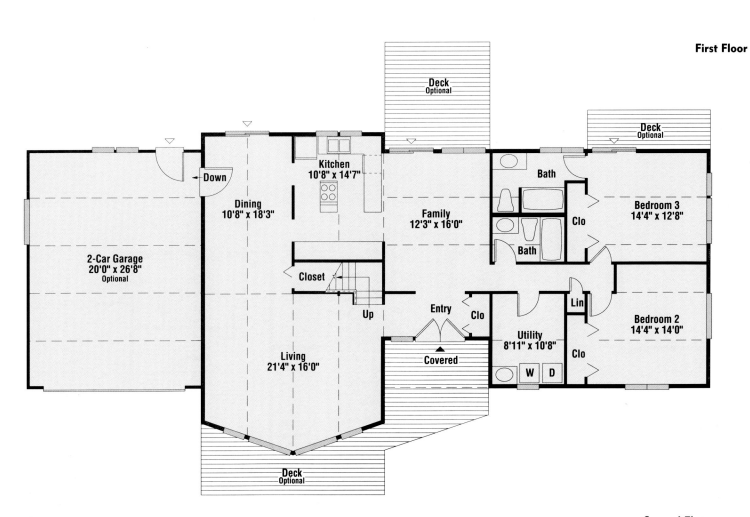

Deck Optional

Kitchen 10'8" x 14'7"

Down

Dining 10'8" x 18'3"

Deck Optional

Bath

Bedroom 3 14'4" x 12'8"

Clo

2-Car Garage 20'0" x 26'8" Optional

Family 12'3" x 16'0"

Bath

Closet

Up

Entry Clo

Lin

Bedroom 2 14'4" x 14'0"

Living 21'4" x 16'0"

Covered

Utility 8'11" x 10'8"

Clo

W D

Deck Optional

Second Floor

Lin

Bath

Master Bedroom Suite 21'4" x 18'3"

Closet

Down

Open to Below

Drywall provides a contrast to the richness of the wood accents in the living room.

Prow Star

RiverVista

- Bedrooms: 3
- Bathrooms: 3
- Master bedroom on second floor
- Total Area: 2023 sq. ft.
- First Floor: 1672 sq. ft.
- Other Floor: 351 sq. ft.
- Size: 59' x 36'
- Entry: Front
- Photos of Prow Stars on pages 84–91.

Prow Star

Mountain Vista

- Bedrooms: 2
- Bathrooms: 2
- Master bedroom on first floor
- Total Area: 2276 sq. ft.
- First Floor: 1992 sq. ft.
- Other Floor: 284 sq. ft.
- Size: 71' x 38'
- Entry: Back
- Photos of Prow Stars on pages 84–91.

First Floor

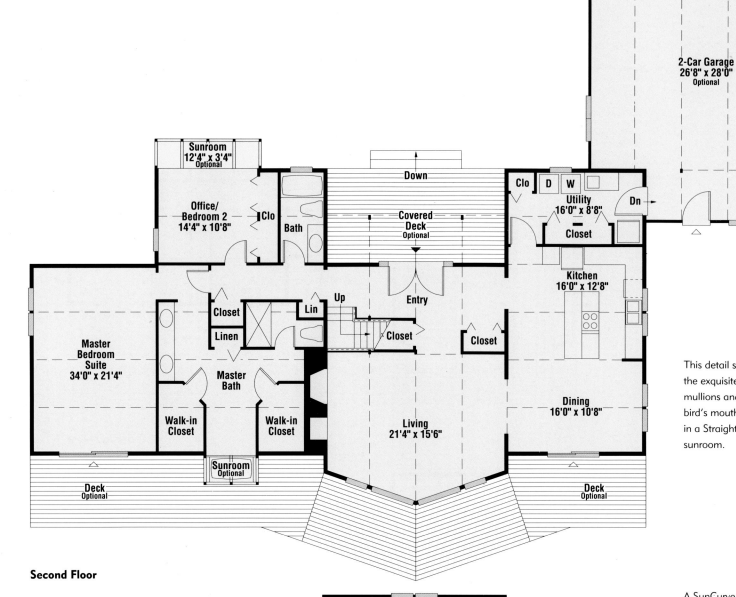

2-Car Garage
26'8" x 28'0"
Optional

Sunroom
12'4" x 3'4"
Optional

Down

Clo D W

Utility
16'0" x 8'8"

Dn

Office/
Bedroom 2
14'4" x 10'8"

Clo

Bath

Covered
Deck
Optional

Closet

Kitchen
16'0" x 12'8"

Up

Entry

Closet

Lin

Closet

Linen

Closet

Master
Bedroom
Suite
34'0" x 21'4"

Master
Bath

Walk-in
Closet

Walk-in
Closet

Sunroom
Optional

Living
21'4" x 15'6"

Dining
16'0" x 10'8"

Deck
Optional

Deck
Optional

Sunroom Options

This detail shows the exquisite cedar mullions and the bird's mouth joinery in a Straight Eave sunroom.

A SunCurve style sunroom could be substituted.

Second Floor

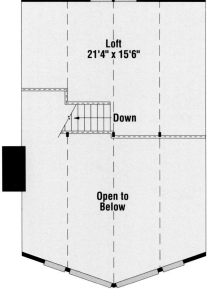

The loft is an appealing getaway. The owners added the windows at the peak.

Loft
21'4" x 15'6"

Down

Open to
Below

© LINDAL CEDAR HOMES

In the BrookVista—unlike most daylight basement homes—bedrooms are on the entry level and living spaces are downstairs.

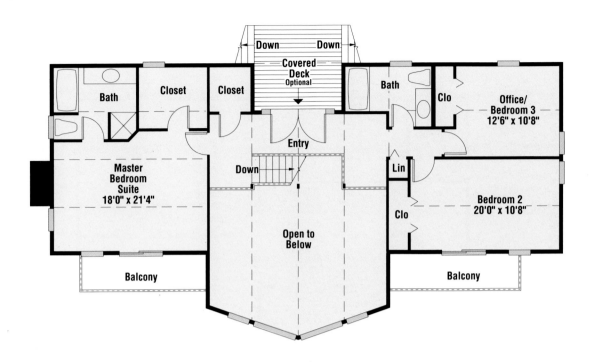

Bath

Closet   Closet

Covered Deck Optional

Bath

Clo

Office/ Bedroom 3
12'6" x 10'8"

Entry

Master Bedroom Suite
18'0" x 21'4"

Down

Lin

Clo

Bedroom 2
20'0" x 10'8"

Open to Below

Balcony

Balcony

Prow Star

BrookVista

- Bedrooms: 3
- Bathrooms: 2 Full & 1 Half
- Master bedroom on first floor
- Total Area: 2404 sq. ft.
- First Floor: 1026 sq. ft.
- Other Floor: 1378 sq. ft.
- Size: 59' x 31'
- Entry: Back
- Photos of Prow Stars on pages 84–91.

A bird's eye view from the entry down to the living room.

Daylight Basement

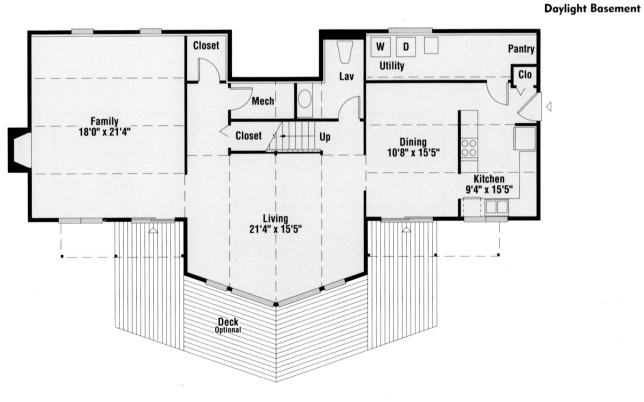

Closet

W D   Pantry

Utility

Lav

Clo

Mech

Family
18'0" x 21'4"

Closet   Up

Dining
10'8" x 15'5"

Kitchen
9'4" x 15'5"

Living
21'4" x 15'5"

Deck Optional

Prow Star with 2 Story Wings

WoodLawn

- Bedrooms: 3
- Bathrooms: 2 Full & 1 Half
- Master bedroom on second floor
- Total Area: 2042 sq. ft.
- First Floor: 1278 sq. ft.
- Other Floor: 764 sq. ft.
- Size: 46' x 38'
- Entry: Front
- Photos of Prow Stars with 2 Story Wings on pages 92–93.

First Floor

Deck
Optional

D
W
Utility
Lav
Kitchen
18'11" x 10'8"
Family
14'0" x 15'6"

Down

2-Car Garage
23'0" x 21'4"
Optional

Closet

Pantry

Closet
Dining
14'6" x 11'9"
Up

Entry

Covered Deck
Optional

Living
21'4" x 20'3"

Second Floor

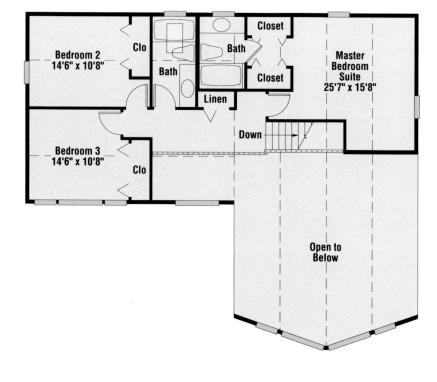

Closet

Bath

Bedroom 2
14'6" x 10'8"
Clo
Bath
Closet

Master Bedroom Suite
25'7" x 15'8"

Linen

Bedroom 3
14'6" x 10'8"
Clo

Down

Open to Below

Glue-laminated beams, wood ceiling liner and cedar framed windows add warm notes in the dining room.

These owners personalized the windows in the prow and added cedar liner diagonally to form a herringbone pattern.

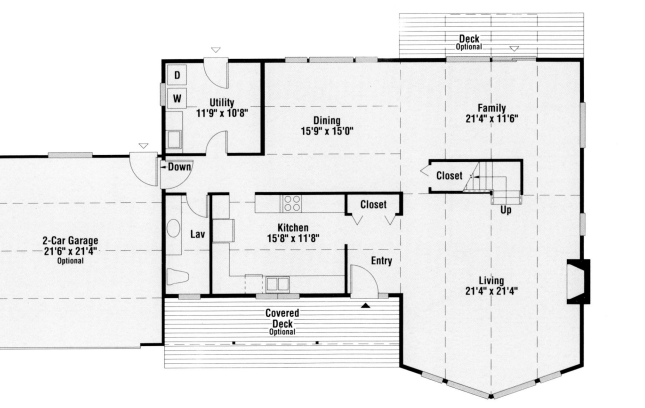

Deck
Optional

Utility
11'9" x 10'8"

D
W

Dining
15'9" x 15'0"

Family
21'4" x 11'6"

Down

Closet

Up

2-Car Garage
21'6" x 21'4"
Optional

Lav

Kitchen
15'8" x 11'8"

Closet

Entry

Living
21'4" x 21'4"

Covered Deck
Optional

Prow Star with 2 Story Wings

WoodGate

- Bedrooms: 4
- Bathrooms: 2 Full & 1 Half
- Master bedroom on second floor
- Total Area: 2539 sq. ft.
- First Floor: 1507 sq. ft.
- Other Floor: 1032 sq. ft.
- Size: 49' x 38'
- Entry: Front
- Photos of Prow Stars with 2 Story Wings on pages 92–93.

Second Floor

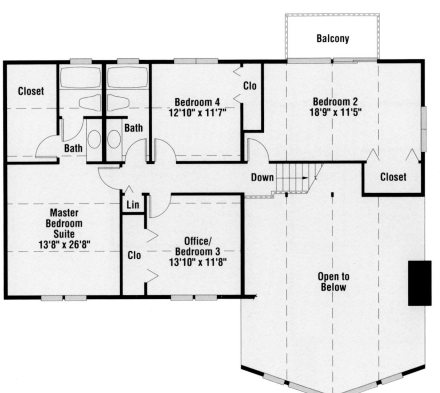

Balcony

Closet

Bedroom 4
12'10" x 11'7"

Clo

Bedroom 2
18'9" x 11'5"

Bath

Bath

Down

Closet

Master Bedroom Suite
13'8" x 26'8"

Lin

Clo

Office/ Bedroom 3
13'10" x 11'8"

Open to Below

Exterior doors come with safety-conscious lockset and deadbolt. Lever hardware is optional.

Prow Star with 1 & 2 Story Wings

WoodLand

- Bedrooms: 4
- Bathrooms: 3 Full & 1 Half
- Master bedroom on second floor
- Total Area: 2551 sq. ft.
- First Floor: 1641 sq. ft.
- Other Floor: 910 sq. ft.
- Size: 57' x 36'
- Entry: Back
- Photos of Prow Stars with 1 & 2 Story Wings on pages 94–95.

First Floor

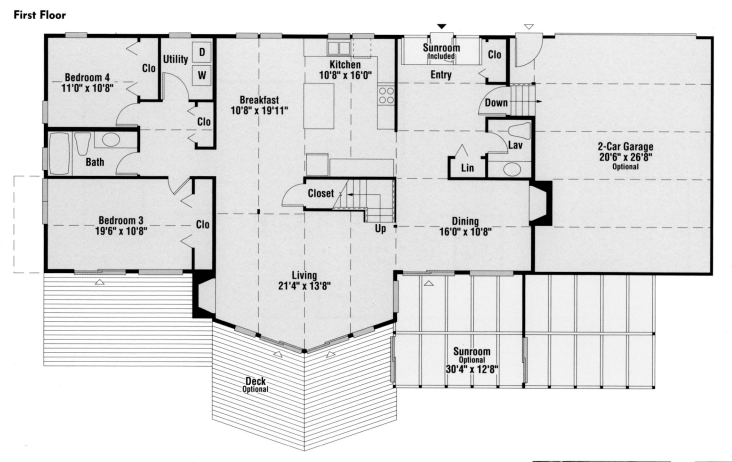

Bedroom 4
11'0" x 10'8"

Clo

Utility

D

W

Clo

Clo

Bath

Bedroom 3
19'6" x 10'8"

Clo

Breakfast
10'8" x 19'11"

Kitchen
10'8" x 16'0"

Sunroom
Included

Clo

Entry

Down

Lav

Lin

Closet

Up

Dining
16'0" x 10'8"

2-Car Garage
20'6" x 26'8"
Optional

Living
21'4" x 13'8"

Deck
Optional

Sunroom
Optional
30'4" x 12'8"

A sliding glass door divides the optional 10-bay sunroom: half is used for a sitting room, and half is for exercise.

Second Floor

Closet

Bath

Clo

Bath

Bath

Master
Bedroom
Suite
19'6" x 26'8"

Closet

Lin

Guest Suite/ Office
21'4" x 16'2"

Down

Balc

Open to
Below

Wood framed sliding glass doors lead to the deck.

With lots of windows and a skylight, the master bedroom is bright and airy.

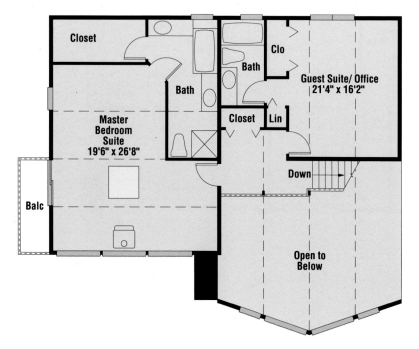

In post and beam architecture, girders and beams add beauty as well as strength.

This spacious kitchen has both an eating bar and a breakfast nook.

© LINDAL CEDAR HOMES

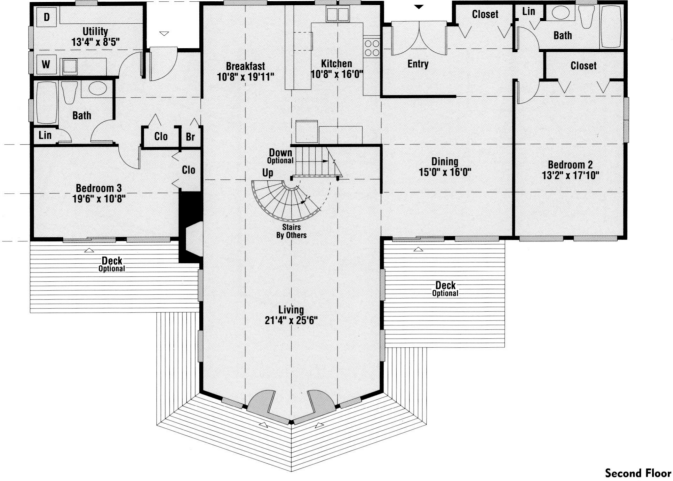

Utility
13'4" x 8'5"

D

W

Bath

Lin

Breakfast
10'8" x 19'11"

Kitchen
10'8" x 16'0"

Entry

Closet

Lin

Bath

Closet

Bedroom 3
19'6" x 10'8"

Clo

Br

Clo

Down
Optional
Up

Stairs
By Others

Dining
15'0" x 16'0"

Bedroom 2
13'2" x 17'10"

Deck
Optional

Deck
Optional

Living
21'4" x 25'6"

Second Floor

Master Bedroom Suite
27'2" x 26'8"

Up

Tower Optional Stairs By Others

Balcony

Bath

Clo

Clo

Office/ Bedroom 4
13'8" x 16'0"

Closet

Down

Open to Below

Arched portals lead to the formal dining room.

Prow Star with 1 & 2 Story Wings

WoodHaven

- Bedrooms: 4
- Bathrooms: 3
- Master bedroom on second floor
- Total Area: 3136 sq. ft.
- First Floor: 2189 sq. ft.
- Other Floor: 947 sq. ft.
- Size: 69' x 47'
- Entry: Back
- Photos of Prow Stars with 1 & 2 Story Wings on pages 94–95.

Note: The owners added the tower as an observatory. Be sure to check with your local building department before proceeding with this option.

Summit Star

NewPort

- Bedrooms: 3
- Bathrooms: 2 Full & 1 Half
- Master bedroom on first floor
- Total Area: 2064 sq. ft.
- First Floor: 1740 sq. ft.
- Other Floor: 324 sq. ft.
- Size: 65' x 38'
- Entry: Back
- Photos of Summit Stars on pages 96–97.

First Floor

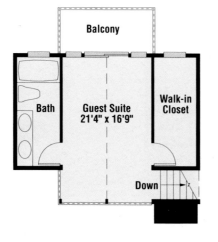

D
W

Lav

Utility
10'8"x12'10"

Entry

Office/
Bedroom 3
16'0" x 12'10"

Bath

Down

Pantry

Lin

Closet

Closet

Master
Bedroom
Suite
20'5" x 21'4"

Closet

Closet

Up

Kitchen
10'8" x 16'6"

Dining
10'8" x 16'0"

Living
21'4" x 14'11"

Down

Deck
Optional

This detail shows
the handsome
oak handle on
the wood framed
sliding glass door.

Second Floor

Balcony

Bath

Guest Suite
21'4" x 16'9"

Walk-in
Closet

Down

Consider a store door as an alternative to a solid panel entry door.

Swinging patio doors hinge together in the center and one folds inward—handles on the side.

French doors hinge on the sides and both open from the middle—handles in the center.

First Floor

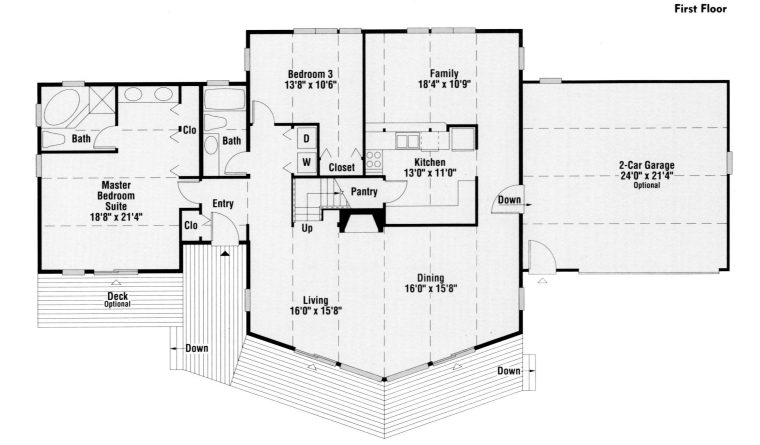

Bedroom 3
13'8" x 10'6"

Family
18'4" x 10'9"

Bath

Clo

Bath

D

W

Closet

Kitchen
13'0" x 11'0"

Pantry

2-Car Garage
24'0" x 21'4"
Optional

Master
Bedroom
Suite
18'8" x 21'4"

Entry

Clo

Up

Down

Dining
16'0" x 15'8"

Deck
Optional

Down

Living
16'0" x 15'8"

Down

Second Floor

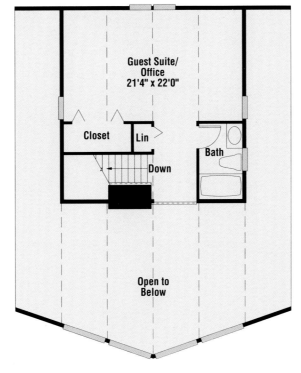

Guest Suite/
Office
21'4" x 22'0"

Closet

Lin

Bath

Down

Open to
Below

Summit Star

WestPort

- Bedrooms: 3
- Bathrooms: 3
- Master bedroom on first floor
- Total Area: 2082 sq. ft.
- First Floor: 1662 sq. ft.
- Other Floor: 420 sq. ft.
- Size: 56' x 39'
- Entry: Front
- Photos of Summit Stars on pages 96–97.

Ranch

Ponderosa

- Bedrooms: 3
- Bathrooms: 2
- Total Area: 1500 sq. ft.
- Size: 43' x 49'
- Entry: Front
- Photos of Ranches on pages 100–101.

Bedroom 2
12'5" x 10'8"

Clo

Kitchen
12'8" x 10'8"

Dining
13'11" x 10'8"

Clo

Bedroom 3
12'5" x 10'5"

Family
7'6" x 8'3"

Screened Porch
Optional

Bath

Living
15'9" x 16'0"

Lin

Closet

Bath

Down
Optional

Entry

Closet

Master Bedroom Suite
16'0" x 22'0"

Deck
Optional

A screened porch
or Garden Room is
ideal for hot climates
where bugs can be
a nuisance.

Ask your consultant
about the new
GardenRoom—an
alternative room
addition idea.

These homeowners customized window and door treatments in their bedroom.

These owners also personalized their roof design.

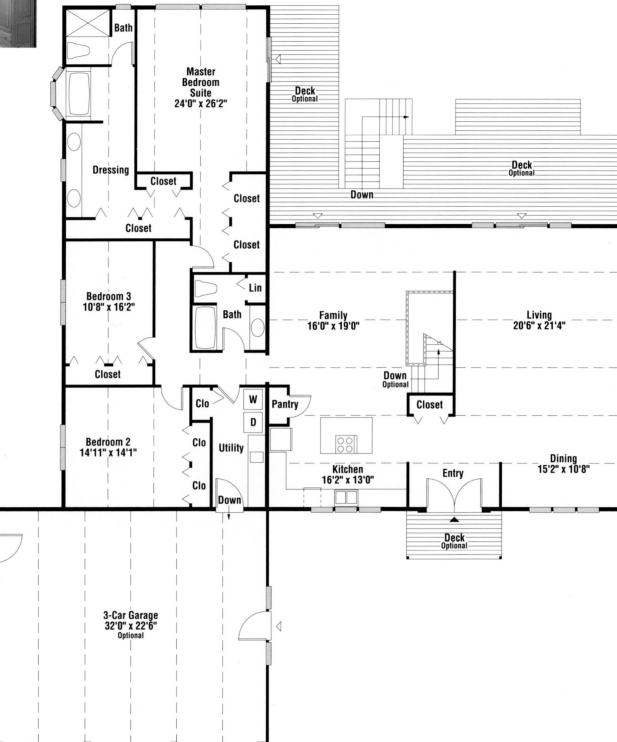

Bath

Master Bedroom Suite
24'0" x 26'2"

Dressing

Closet

Closet

Closet

Closet

Deck
Optional

Deck
Optional

Down

Lin

Bedroom 3
10'8" x 16'2"

Bath

Family
16'0" x 19'0"

Living
20'6" x 21'4"

Closet

Closet

Down
Optional

Closet

Clo

W

D

Pantry

Bedroom 2
14'11" x 14'1"

Clo

Utility

Clo

Kitchen
16'2" x 13'0"

Entry

Dining
15'2" x 10'8"

Down

Deck
Optional

3-Car Garage
32'0" x 22'6"
Optional

Ranch

Silverado

- Bedrooms: 3
- Bathrooms: 2
- Total Area: 2700 sq. ft.
- Size: 66' x 56'
- Entry: Front
- Photos of Ranches on pages 100–101.

Split Level

Tuscany

- Bedrooms: 3
- Bathrooms: 2
- Master bedroom on second floor
- Total Area: 1616 sq. ft.
- First Floor: 1035 sq. ft.
- Other Floor: 581 sq. ft.
- Size: 37' x 31'
- Entry: Back
- Photos of Split Levels on pages 102–103.

First Floor

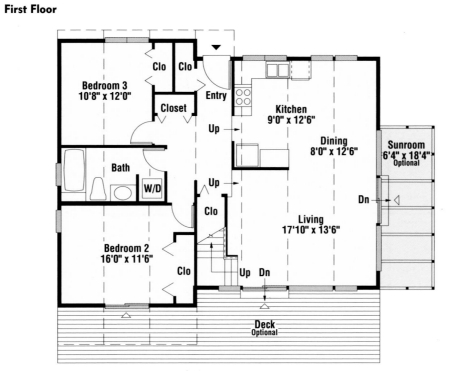

Bedroom 3
10'8" x 12'0"

Clo Clo

Entry

Closet

Kitchen
9'0" x 12'6"

Dining
8'0" x 12'6"

Sunroom
6'4" x 18'4"
Optional

Bath

W/D

Up

Up

Clo

Dn

Living
17'10" x 13'6"

Bedroom 2
16'0" x 11'6"

Clo

Up Dn

Deck
Optional

Instead of a sunroom,
the owners opted for
a screened porch.

Second Floor

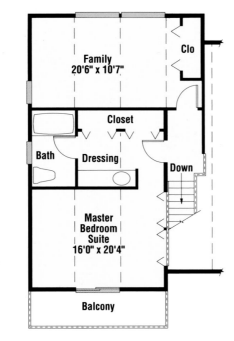

Family
20'6" x 10'7"

Clo

Closet

Bath

Dressing

Down

Master
Bedroom
Suite
16'0" x 20'4"

Balcony

Cedar decking with
simple rail.

In the Bavaria, the living room projects on the right and the breakfast room on the left.

From the family room it's half a dozen steps down to the more formal and separate living room.

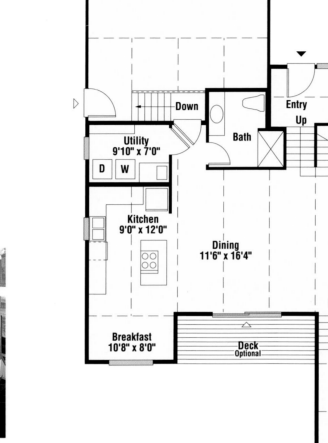

2-Car Garage
21'4" x 21'6"
Included

Down

Entry
Up

Clo

Office
10'1" x 13'0"

Clo

Bath

Utility
9'10" x 7'0"

D W

Kitchen
9'0" x 12'0"

Dining
11'6" x 16'4"

Family
21'4" x 15'0"

Down

Breakfast
10'8" x 8'0"

Deck
Optional

Living
16'0" x 16'0"

Down

Deck
Optional

Down

Closet

Bath

Bedroom 2
21'4" x 14'6"

Open to Below

Clo

Bath

Closet

Down

Closet

Master Bedroom Suite
26'8" x 12'1"

Split Level

Bavaria

- Bedrooms: 2 + Office
- Bathrooms:
  2 Full & 1 Three-quarter
- Master bedroom on second floor
- Total Area: 2167 sq. ft.
- First Floor: 1403 sq. ft.
- Other Floor: 764 sq. ft.
- Size: 43' x 44'
- Entry: Back
- Photos of Split Levels on pages 102–103.

College

Harvard

- Bedrooms: 3
- Bathrooms: 2 Full & 1 Half
- Master bedroom on second floor
- Total Area: 2393 sq. ft.
- First Floor: 1535 sq. ft.
- Other Floor: 858 sq. ft.
- Size: 53' x 43'
- Entry: Back
- Photos of Colleges on pages 104–105.

First Floor

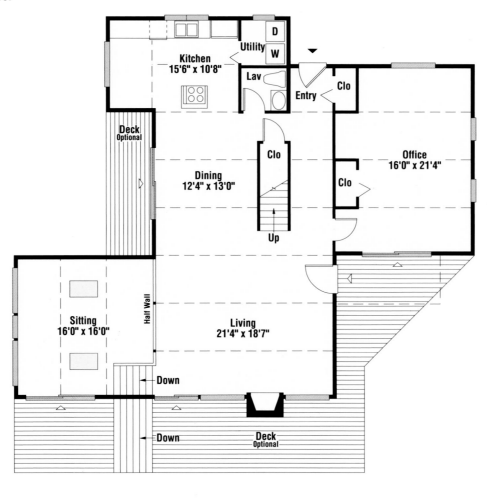

Kitchen 15'6" x 10'8"

Utility

D
W

Lav

Entry

Clo

Deck Optional

Dining 12'4" x 13'0"

Clo

Clo

Office 16'0" x 21'4"

Clo

Up

Half Wall

Sitting 16'0" x 16'0"

Living 21'4" x 18'7"

Down

Down

Deck Optional

Second Floor

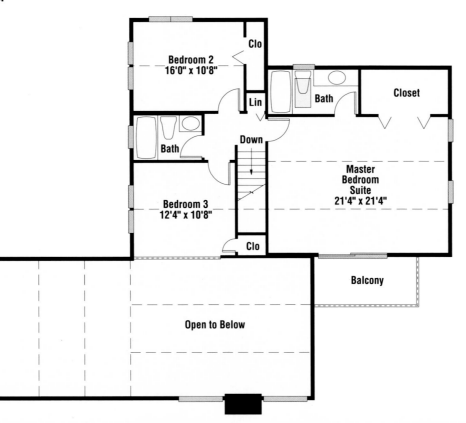

Bedroom 2 16'0" x 10'8"

Clo

Lin

Bath

Closet

Bath

Down

Master Bedroom Suite 21'4" x 21'4"

Bedroom 3 12'4" x 10'8"

Clo

Balcony

Open to Below

Zoning puts the sitting room/study on a lower level.

These owners added astral glass for even more natural light.

And when it comes time to relax, there's nothing like your own front porch.

© LINDAL CEDAR HOMES

A skywall over a 3-foot basewall in the dining room is included in the Princeton.

First Floor

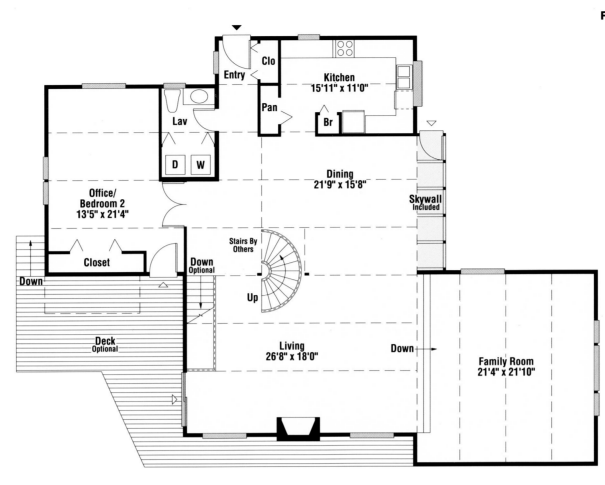

Clo

Entry

Kitchen
15'11" x 11'0"

Pan

Br

Lav

D W

Office/
Bedroom 2
13'5" x 21'4"

Closet

Dining
21'9" x 15'8"

Skywall
Included

Down

Down
Optional

Stairs By
Others

Up

Living
26'8" x 18'0"

Down

Family Room
21'4" x 21'10"

Deck
Optional

A spacious retreat, the master bedroom has generous closets: you can never have enough.

Second Floor

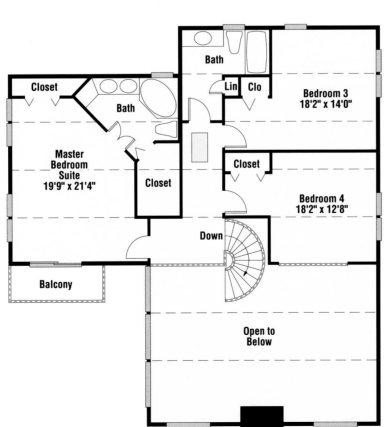

Bath

Closet

Bath

Lin Clo

Bedroom 3
18'2" x 14'0"

Master
Bedroom
Suite
19'9" x 21'4"

Closet

Closet

Bedroom 4
18'2" x 12'8"

Down

Balcony

Open to
Below

College

Princeton

- Bedrooms: 4
- Bathrooms: 2 Full & 1 Half
- Master bedroom on second floor
- Total Area: 3057 sq. ft.
- First Floor: 2040 sq. ft.
- Other Floor: 1017 sq. ft.
- Size: 64' x 48'
- Entry: Back
- Photos of Colleges on pages 104–105.

A soaring cathedral ceiling makes the living room special.

Pavilion

Starlight

- Bedrooms: 4
- Bathrooms: 2 Full & 1 Half
- Master bedroom on first floor
- Total Area: 3024 sq. ft.
- First Floor: 2152 sq. ft.
- Other Floor: 872 sq. ft.
- Size: 69' x 46'
- Entry: Front
- Photos of Pavilions on pages 106–107.

First Floor

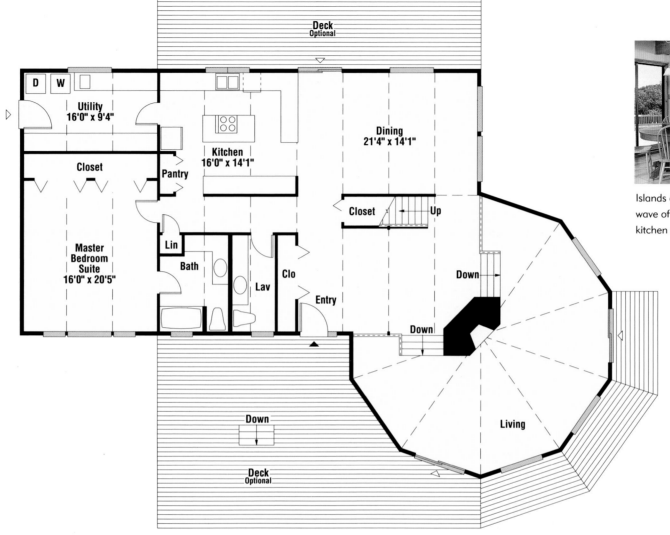

Deck
Optional

D   W

Utility
16'0" x 9'4"

Dining
21'4" x 14'1"

Kitchen
16'0" x 14'1"

Closet

Pantry

Closet   Up

Down

Master
Bedroom
Suite
16'0" x 20'5"

Lin

Bath

Lav

Clo

Entry

Down

Down

Living

Down

Deck
Optional

Islands are riding a
wave of popularity in
kitchen design today.

Second Floor

Bedroom 4
16'0" x 14'1"

Clo Clo

Bedroom 2
21'4" x 14'1"

Open to
Below

Bath

Down

Lin

Clo

Bedroom 3
21'4" x 10'2"

Open to
Below

A many sided pavilion
is the dramatic focal
point of this design.

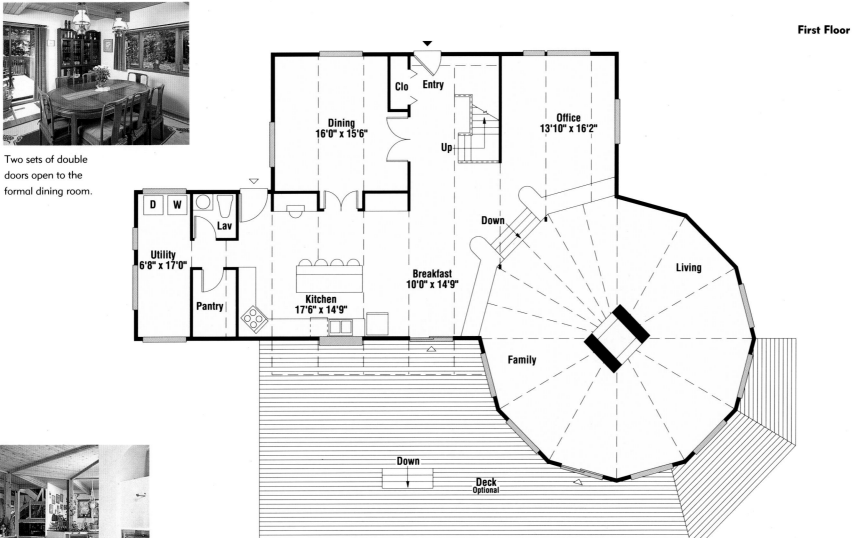

Two sets of double
doors open to the
formal dining room.

Dining
16'0" x 15'6"

Clo

Entry

Up

Office
13'10" x 16'2"

Down

Living

D **W**

Lav

Utility
6'8" x 17'0"

Pantry

Kitchen
17'6" x 14'9"

Breakfast
10'0" x 14'9"

Family

Down

Deck
Optional

The fireplace divides
the sunken pavilion
into cozier areas.

Pavilion

Stargazer

- Bedrooms: 4
- Bathrooms: 2 Full & 1 Half
- Master bedroom on second floor
- Total Area: 3589 sq. ft.
- First Floor: 2181 sq. ft.
- Other Floor: 1408 sq. ft.
- Size: 73' x 49'
- Entry: Back
- Photos of Pavilions on
  pages 106–107.

Second Floor

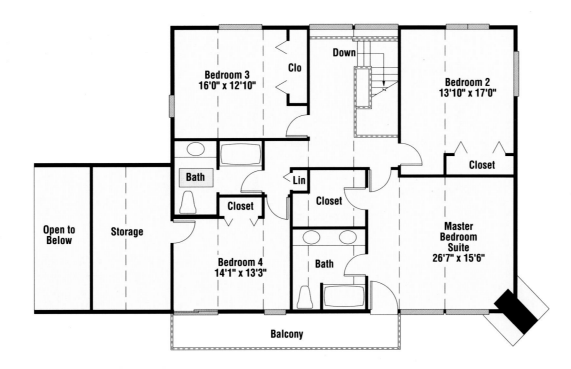

Bedroom 3
16'0" x 12'10"

Clo

Down

Bedroom 2
13'10" x 17'0"

Bath

Lin

Closet

Closet

**Open to
Below**

Storage

Closet

Closet

**Master
Bedroom
Suite**
26'7" x 15'6"

Bedroom 4
14'1" x 13'3"

Bath

Balcony

Executive

Georgetown

- Bedrooms: 3
- Bathrooms: 1 Full,
  1 Three-quarter & 1 Half
- Master bedroom on first floor
- Total Area: 2226 sq. ft.
- First Floor: 1622 sq. ft.
- Other Floor: 604 sq. ft.
- Size: 64' x 32'
- Entry: Front
- Photos of Executives on
  pages 108–109.

First Floor

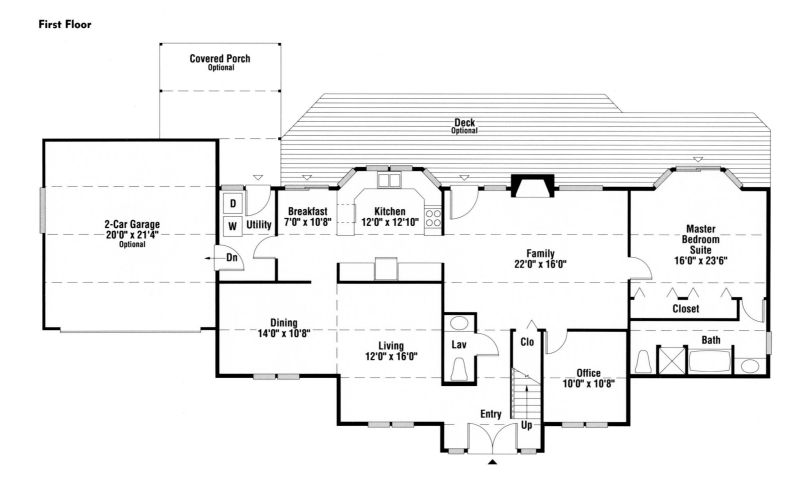

Covered Porch
Optional

Deck
Optional

2-Car Garage
20'0" x 21'4"
Optional

D

D
W **Utility**

Dn

Breakfast
7'0" x 10'8"

Kitchen
12'0" x 12'10"

Family
22'0" x 16'0"

**Master
Bedroom
Suite**
16'0" x 23'6"

Closet

Bath

Dining
14'0" x 10'8"

Living
12'0" x 16'0"

Lav

Clo

Office
10'0" x 10'8"

Entry

Up

The master bedroom
suite is generously
sized, with closets
forming a sound bar-
rier between sleeping
and bath areas.

Second Floor

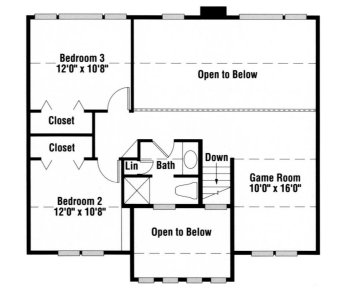

The foyer is formal
with a cathedral
ceiling above. The
owners added even
more windows here
and elsewhere.

Bedroom 3
12'0" x 10'8"

Open to Below

Closet

Closet

Lin **Bath** **Down**

Game Room
10'0" x 16'0"

Bedroom 2
12'0" x 10'8"

Open to Below

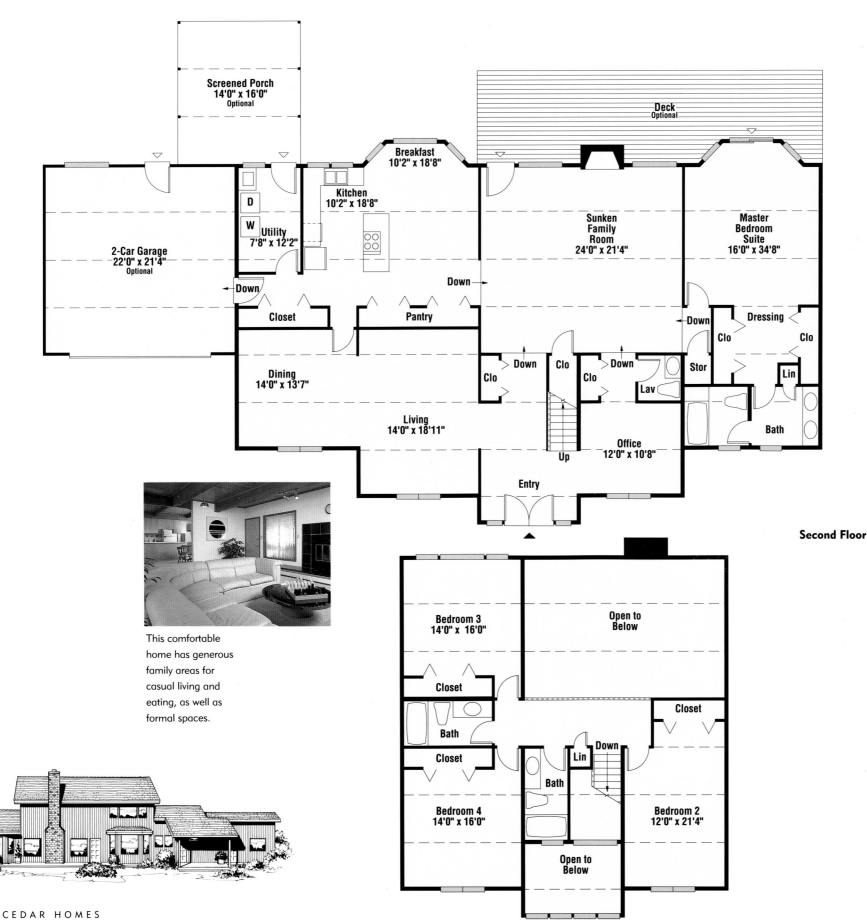

Screened Porch
14'0" x 16'0"
Optional

Deck
Optional

Breakfast
10'2" x 18'8"

Kitchen
10'2" x 18'8"

2-Car Garage
22'0" x 21'4"
Optional

D

W

Utility
7'8" x 12'2"

Sunken
Family
Room
24'0" x 21'4"

Master
Bedroom
Suite
16'0" x 34'8"

Down

Closet

Pantry

Dressing

Down

Clo

Clo

Down

Clo

Down

Stor

Lin

Dining
14'0" x 13'7"

Clo

Clo

Clo

Lav

Living
14'0" x 18'11"

Bath

Office
12'0" x 10'8"

Up

Entry

Executive

Scarsdale

- Bedrooms: 4
- Bathrooms: 3 Full & 1 Half
- Master bedroom on first floor
- Total Area: 3399 sq. ft.
- First Floor: 2466 sq. ft.
- Other Floor: 933 sq. ft.
- Size: 68' x 43'
- Entry: Front
- Photos of Executives on
  pages 108–109.

This comfortable
home has generous
family areas for
casual living and
eating, as well as
formal spaces.

Second Floor

Bedroom 3
14'0" x 16'0"

Open to
Below

Closet

Closet

Bath

Closet

Closet

Lin

Down

Bath

Bedroom 4
14'0" x 16'0"

Bedroom 2
12'0" x 21'4"

Open to
Below

City

Hillsborough

- Bedrooms: 3
- Bathrooms: 2 Full & 1 Half
- Master bedroom on second floor
- Total Area: 1726 sq. ft.
- First Floor: 998 sq. ft.
- Other Floor: 728 sq. ft.
- Size: 35' x 33'
- Entry: Front
- Photos of Cities on pages 110–111.

Designed for a narrow urban lot, this home presents a private face to the street and opens to the view in the back.

First Floor

Second Floor

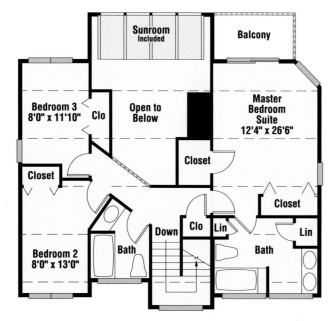

Positioning the sunroom (included) over opening doors of a matching width, makes a dramatic statement.

The owners chose to paint all surfaces—including wood—for a cool, urban look.

© LINDAL CEDAR HOMES

Second Floor

Sunroom
Included

Balcony

Open to Below

Bedroom 2
11'0" x 16'0"

Master
Bedroom
Suite
16'6" x 26'8"

Closet

Bath

Sitting
12'6" x 10'8"

Lin

Bath

Bedroom 3
14'0" x 10'8"

Clo

Down

Open to Below

Closet

Shelf

First Floor

Deck
Optional

Living
15'6" x 21'4"

Down

Bedroom 4
11'0" x 16'0"

Dining
16'6" x 12'6"

Down

Kitchen
12'4" x 10'6"

Closet

Clo

Bath

Clo

Up

Clo

Breakfast
12'4" x 10'2"

W

D

Utility

Down

Entry

Clo

Sunroom
Included

Deck
Optional

2-Car Garage
21'4" x 21'4"
Optional

Inside, the home
opens up to its view.
A 4-bay sunroom
(included) tops two
pairs of swinging
patio doors—the
owners' choice.

A 4-bay sunroom
with glass end wall
(included) adds space
for a breakfast room.

City

Westchester

- Bedrooms: 4
- Bathrooms: 3
- Master bedroom on second floor
- Total Area: 2443 sq. ft.
- First Floor: 1447 sq. ft.
- Other Floor: 996 sq. ft.
- Size: 43' x 38'
- Entry: Front
- Photos of Cities on pages 110–111.

The owners moved
their upstairs balcony
to Bedroom 2, and
added a round
window in the
garage wall.

Signature

Landmark

- Bedrooms: 3
- Bathrooms: 2
- Master bedroom on second floor
- Total Area: 1937 sq. ft.
- First Floor: 1255 sq. ft.
- Other Floor: 682 sq. ft.
- Size: 43' x 32'
- Entry: Front
- Photos of Signatures on pages 112–113.

First Floor

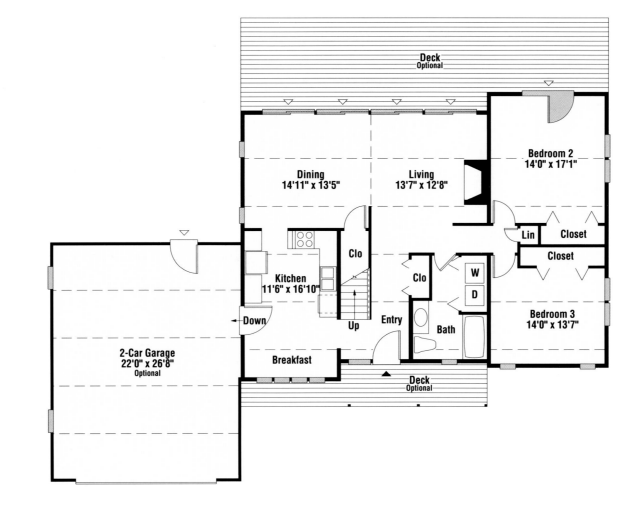

Dining 14'11" x 13'5"

Living 13'7" x 12'8"

Bedroom 2 14'0" x 17'1"

Kitchen 11'6" x 16'10"

Clo

Lin   Closet

Clo   Closet

W
D

Bedroom 3 14'0" x 13'7"

Down   **Up**   **Entry**   **Bath**

2-Car Garage 22'0" x 26'8" Optional

Breakfast

Deck Optional

Deck Optional

In the living and dining rooms, sunwall units top sliding glass doors to maximize the view.

Second Floor

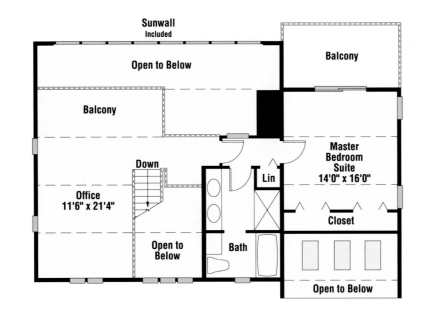

Sunwall Included

Open to Below

Balcony

Balcony

Down

Office 11'6" x 21'4"

Master Bedroom Suite 14'0" x 16'0"

Lin

Bath

Closet

Open to Below

Open to Below

Open to Below

A family-size dining room with easy access to the deck—and the barbecue.

From the living room, there's a view up to the open rail bridge joining the 2 wings.

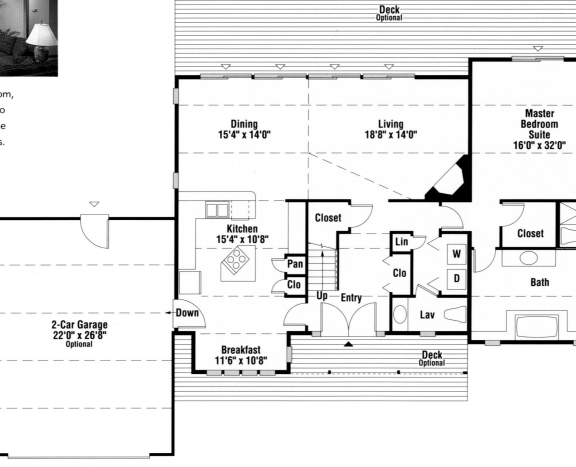

First Floor

Deck
Optional

Dining
15'4" x 14'0"

Living
18'8" x 14'0"

Master
Bedroom
Suite
16'0" x 32'0"

Kitchen
15'4" x 10'8"

Closet

Closet

Bath

Pan

Lin

W

Clo

Clo

D

2-Car Garage
22'0" x 26'8"
Optional

Down

Up

Entry

Lav

Breakfast
11'6" x 10'8"
Optional

Deck
Optional

Relocating the garage allowed more windows in the kitchen—and encouraged a complete kitchen redesign.

Second Floor

Sunwall
Included

Game Room
15'4" x 10'8"

Open to Below

Balcony

Closet

Closet

Bedroom 3
16'0" x 11'2"

Closet

Down

Lin

Open to Below

Bedroom 2
15'4" x 16'0"

Open to
Below

Bath

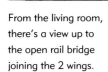

Signature

Hallmark

- Bedrooms: 3
- Bathrooms: 2 Full & 1 Half
- Master bedroom on first floor
- Total Area: 2346 sq. ft.
- First Floor: 1548 sq. ft.
- Other Floor: 798 sq. ft.
- Size: 50' x 35'
- Entry: Front
- Photos of Signatures on pages 112–113.

With a sloping site, the owners positioned their garage under the house instead of to the side.

Designer

Sundowner

- Bedrooms: 3
- Bathrooms: 2
- Master bedroom on second floor
- Total Area: 2020 sq. ft.
- First Floor: 1429 sq. ft.
- Other Floor: 591 sq. ft.
- Size: 51' x 32'
- Entry: Front
- Photos of Designers on pages 114–119.

The owners chose to have the two-car garage open to the street rather than to the side.

First Floor

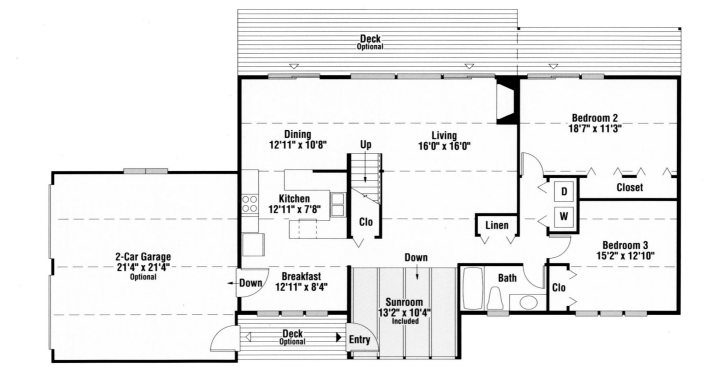

Three clerestory windows flood the kitchen and dining areas with lots of light.

Second Floor

A 4-bay sunroom (included) makes a charming entry to the home.

A quartet of cedar framed glass rectangles forms a window wall to the view.

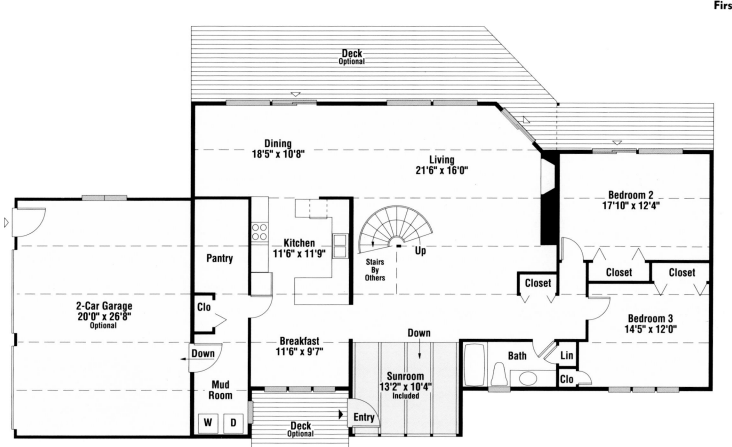

Deck
Optional

Dining
18'5" x 10'8"

Living
21'6" x 16'0"

Bedroom 2
17'10" x 12'4"

Kitchen
11'6" x 11'9"

Pantry

Stairs
By
Others

Up

Closet

Closet

Closet

2-Car Garage
20'0" x 26'8"
Optional

Clo

Down

Breakfast
11'6" x 9'7"

Down

Bedroom 3
14'5" x 12'0"

Mud
Room

W   D

Sunroom
13'2" x 10'4"
Included

Bath

Lin

Clo

Deck
Optional

Entry

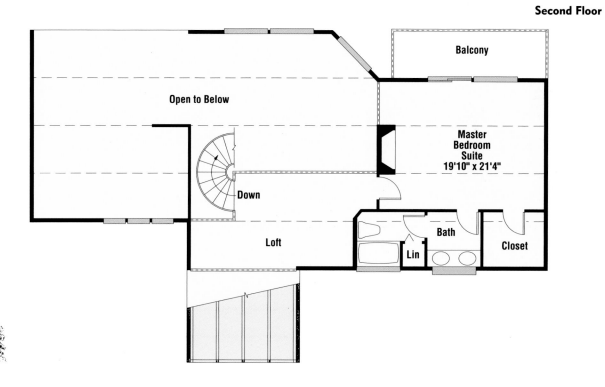

Balcony

Open to Below

Master
Bedroom
Suite
19'10" x 21'4"

Down

Loft

Bath

Lin

Closet

The master suite has a walk-in closet, compartmentalized bath—and a private balcony.

Designer

Sunburst

- Bedrooms: 3
- Bathrooms: 2
- Master bedroom on second floor
- Total Area: 2542 sq. ft.
- First Floor: 1906 sq. ft.
- Other Floor: 636 sq. ft.
- Size: 60' x 37'
- Entry: Front
- Photos of Designers on
  pages 114–119.

Cape

Cape Breton

- Bedrooms: 3
- Bathrooms:
  2 Full & 1 Three-quarter
- Master bedroom on first floor
- Total Area: 2533 sq. ft.
- First Floor: 1863 sq. ft.
- Other Floor: 670 sq. ft.
- Size: 62' x 34'
- Entry: Front
- Photos of Capes on page 122.

First Floor

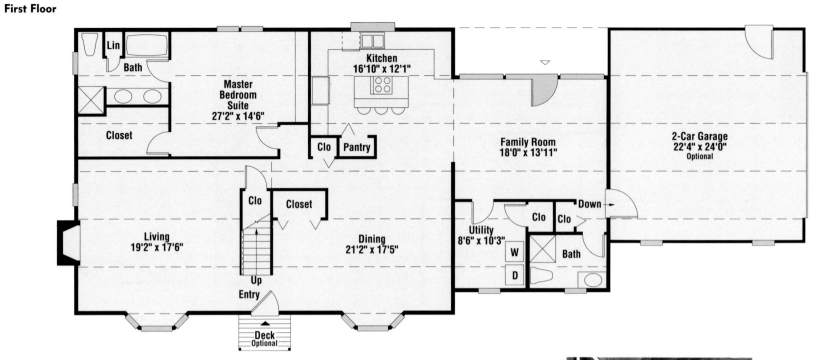

Lin

Bath

Master
Bedroom
Suite
27'2" x 14'6"

Kitchen
16'10" x 12'1"

Closet

2-Car Garage
22'4" x 24'0"
Optional

Clo Pantry

Family Room
18'0" x 13'11"

Clo Closet

Down

Living
19'2" x 17'6"

Dining
21'2" x 17'5"

Utility
8'6" x 10'3"

Clo Clo

W

Bath

D

Up
Entry

Deck
Optional

Second Floor

Bath

Bedroom 2
19'0" x 16'0"

Clo

Lin

Clo

Office/
Bedroom 3
16'9" x 16'0"

Clo

Down

Loft
21'4" x 5'4"

Open to
Below

Upstairs there's an
open rail bridge and
3 dormers for an
open, airy feeling.

Tudor

Cotswold

- Bedrooms: 4
- Bathrooms: 2 & 1 Half
- Master bedroom on second floor
- Total Area: 3075 sq. ft.
- First Floor: 1340 sq. ft.
- Other Floor: 1735 sq. ft.
- Size: 54' x 43'
- Entry: Front
- Photos of Tudors on page 123.

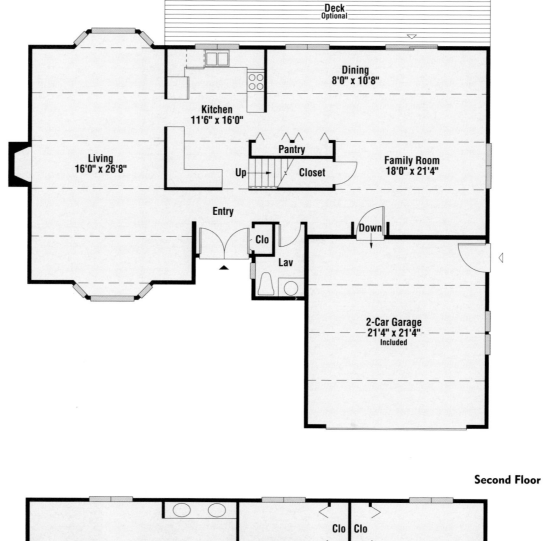

Deck
Optional

Dining
8'0" x 10'8"

Kitchen
11'6" x 16'0"

Pantry

Living
16'0" x 26'8"

Up **Closet**

Family Room
18'0" x 21'4"

Entry

Down

Clo

Lav

2-Car Garage
21'4" x 21'4"
Included

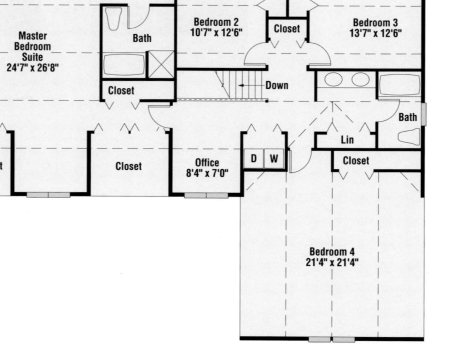

Second Floor

Master Bedroom Suite
24'7" x 26'8"

Bath

Clo Clo

Bedroom 2
10'7" x 12'6"

Closet

Bedroom 3
13'7" x 12'6"

Closet

Down

Bath

Lin

Closet

Closet

Office
8'4" x 7'0"

D W

Closet

Bedroom 4
21'4" x 21'4"

Composite shingles with a 25-year guarantee are standard.

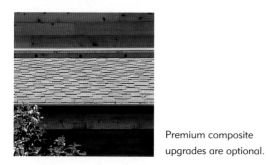

Premium composite upgrades are optional.

Thickbutt, handsplit, resawn No. 1 grade cedar shakes are a deluxe option.

PLANS
TRADITIONAL

Heritage

Hancock

- Bedrooms: 3
- Bathrooms: 2
- Master bedroom on second floor
- Total Area: 1578 sq. ft.
- First Floor: 981 sq. ft.
- Other Floor: 597 sq. ft.
- Size: 37' x 30'
- Entry: Side
- Photos of Heritages on page 124.

The owners added a dormer on the right, and changed some windows and doors to suit themselves.

First Floor

Bath

Clo

Bedroom 3
11'9" x 10'8"

Linen

D

W

Family
16'0" x 21'4"

Kitchen
8'0" x 9'8"

Closet

Up

Entry

Dining
10'8" x 9'7"

Living
10'8" x 15'9"

Deck
Optional

Second Floor

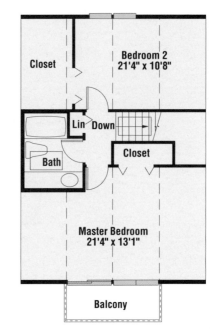

Closet

Bedroom 2
21'4" x 10'8"

Lin Down

Bath

Closet

Master Bedroom
21'4" x 13'1"

Balcony

A Polar Cap II roof system (R-63) is the ultimate in roof insulation.

Put a skylight over a staircase, in a hall— or anywhere you want more light.

Office
12'0" x 12'2"

Dining
14'8" x 12'2"

Kitchen
14'0" x 10'8"

Down

W

D

2-Car Garage
22'0" x 21'4"
Optional

Closet

Up

Bath

Family
14'0" x 10'8"

Entry

Living
21'4" x 15'0"

Deck
Optional

Closet

Ceilings in rooms
on the first floor of
2-story homes fea-
ture glue-laminated
beams and wood
ceiling planks.

A detail of the beam
meeting the side wall
and the wood ceiling
planks above.

Heritage

Yorktown

- Bedrooms: 3 + Office
- Bathrooms: 2 Full &
  1 Three-quarter
- Master bedroom on second floor
- Total Area: 2151 sq. ft.
- First Floor: 1334 sq. ft.
- Other Floor: 817 sq. ft.
- Size: 47' x 34'
- Entry: Side
- Photos of Heritages on page 124.

Second Floor

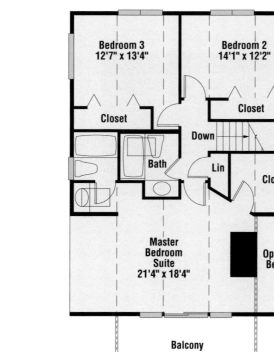

Bedroom 3
12'7" x 13'4"

Bedroom 2
14'1" x 12'2"

Closet

Closet

Down

Bath

Lin

Closet

Master
Bedroom
Suite
21'4" x 18'4"

Open to
Below

Balcony

Colonial

Mayflower

- Bedrooms: 3
- Bathrooms: 2
- Master bedroom on second floor
- Total Area: 1907 sq. ft.
- First Floor: 1392 sq. ft.
- Other Floor: 515 sq. ft.
- Size: 48' x 35'
- Entry: Back
- Photos of Colonials on page 125.

First Floor

Bedroom 2
10'8" x 13'8"

Bath

Bedroom 3
10'8" x 13'8"

Entry

Clo

Closet

Closet

Closet

Living
21'6" x 21'4"

Screened Porch
Optional

D   W

Lin   Up

Kitchen
10'8" x 15'7"

Dining
16'0" x 14'5"

Deck
Optional

Second Floor

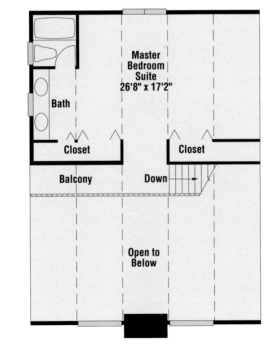

Master
Bedroom
Suite
26'8" x 17'2"

Bath

Closet

Closet

Balcony

Down

Open to
Below

Don't let insects keep
you indoors in sum-
mer. Build a screened
porch with tongue
and groove wood roof
planks and decking—
or consider the new
GardenRoom.

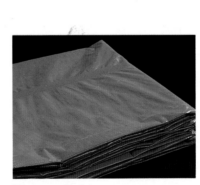

When your Lindal
home package
is delivered, there's
a handy tarp to help
cover your valuable
materials.

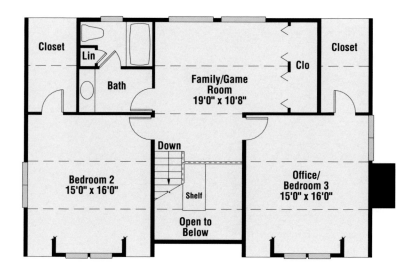

Second Floor plan labels:
Closet — Lin — Bath — Clo — Closet
Family/Game Room 19'0" x 10'8"
Down
Shelf
Bedroom 2 15'0" x 16'0"
Office/Bedroom 3 15'0" x 16'0"
Open to Below

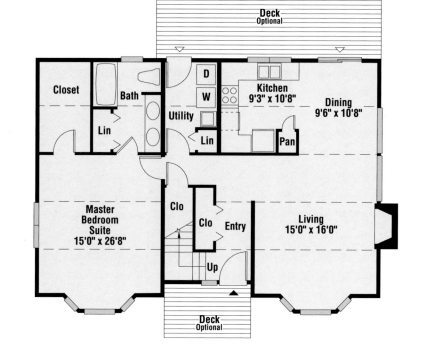

First Floor plan labels:
Deck Optional
Closet — Bath — Utility — Lin
D — W — Kitchen 9'3" x 10'8" — Dining 9'6" x 10'8" — Pan
Master Bedroom Suite 15'0" x 26'8"
Clo — Clo — Entry — Living 15'0" x 16'0"
Up
Deck Optional

New England

Patriot

- Bedrooms: 3
- Bathrooms: 2
- Master bedroom on first floor
- Total Area: 2033 sq. ft.
- First Floor: 1075 sq. ft.
- Other Floor: 958 sq. ft.
- Size: 40' x 28'
- Entry: Front
- Photos of New Englands on pages 126–127

Awnings open from the bottom— permitting ventilation, even when it's raining outside.

Casements open from the sides. All opening windows are equipped with hardware, screen, flashing and trim.

Double hung windows. Both halves move up and down. Removable grids are available. Custom order in fir.

A Palladian or fan window crowns two casements with grids. Custom order in fir.

New England

Whaler

- Bedrooms: 4
- Bathrooms: 2 Full & 1 Half
- Master bedroom on second floor
- Total Area: 2327 sq. ft.
- First Floor: 1184 sq. ft.
- Other Floor: 1143 sq. ft.
- Size: 37' x 32'
- Entry: Front
- Photos of New Englands on pages 126–127.

First Floor

The owners painted their beams and trim to blend with their traditional decor.

Kitchen 16'4" x 14'9"

W/D

Utility

Breezeway Optional

Down

Down

2-Car Garage 22'0" x 26'8" Optional

Dining 13'2" x 14'9"

Closet

Lin

Down

Clo

Sunroom 12'4" x 18'4" Optional

Lav

Deck Optional

Down

Clo

Clo

Living 13'2" x 17'3"

Family 20'4" x 17'3"

Down

Up
Down

Entry

Second Floor

A 2-story sunroom is an appealing option in this plan.

Clo

Bath

Bath

Clo

Bedroom 4 15'3" x 10'8"

Lin

Balcony

Master Bedroom Suite 13'2" x 32'0"

Down

Clo

Office/ Bedroom 3 14'8" x 9'10"

Clo

Clo

Closet

Bedroom 2 20'7" x 11'6"

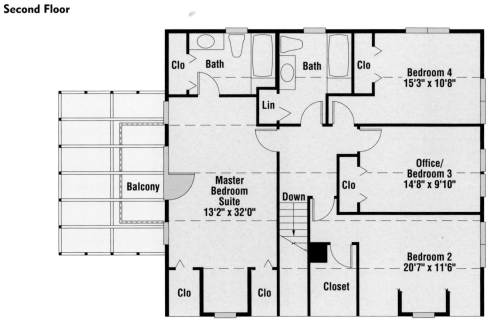

First Floor

Bifolds are available in flush, raised panel and louvre styles, with attractive, solid door pulls.

Our standard passage doors (single and double) are solid core Red oak with handsome premium grade hardware.

Second Floor

Liberty

Independence

- Bedrooms: 3
- Bathrooms: 2
- Master bedroom on first floor
- Total Area: 1614 sq. ft.
- First Floor: 938 sq. ft.
- Other Floor: 676 sq. ft.
- Size: 42' x 23'
- Entry: Back
- Photos of Liberties on page 128.

Liberty

Revere

- Bedrooms: 3
- Bathrooms: 3
- Master bedroom on second floor
- Total Area: 2172 sq. ft.
- First Floor: 1231 sq. ft.
- Other Floor: 941 sq. ft.
- Size: 45' x 27'
- Entry: Front
- Photos of Liberties on page 128.

First Floor

- 2-Car Garage
  28'0" x 21'4"
  Optional
- Bath
- Up
- Clo
- Clo
- Family
  14'10" x 10'8"
- Pantry
- D W
- Utility
  Optional
- Down
- Kitchen
  14'11" x 16'0"
- Office
  10'7" x 16'0"
- Entry
- Living
  14'10" x 16'0"
- Dining
  14'11" x 10'8"

Second Floor

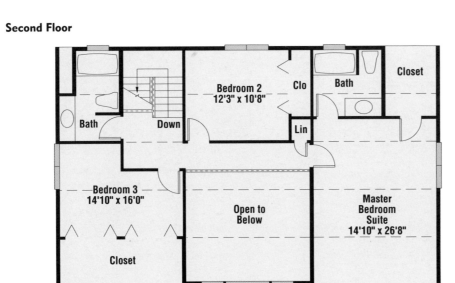

- Bath
- Down
- Bedroom 2
  12'3" x 10'8"
- Clo
- Bath
- Closet
- Lin
- Bedroom 3
  14'10" x 16'0"
- Open to
  Below
- Master
  Bedroom
  Suite
  14'10" x 26'8"
- Closet

These are examples of connectors that are provided for standard load conditions. Engineering for your specific requirements may increase size and cost of connectors.

Optional raised panel cedar garage doors add a deluxe finishing touch.

Relax on your deck.
You deserve it!

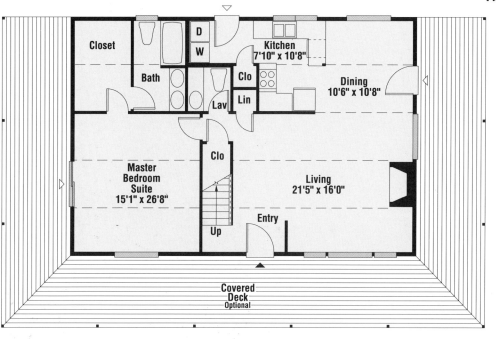

Closet

D
W

Kitchen
7'10" x 10'8"

Bath

Clo
Lin

Dining
10'6" x 10'8"

Lav

Clo

Master
Bedroom
Suite
15'1" x 26'8"

Up

Entry

Living
21'5" x 16'0"

Covered
Deck
Optional

Farmhouse

Pioneer

- Bedrooms: 3
- Bathrooms: 2 Full & 1 Half
- Master bedroom on first floor
- Total Area: 1867 sq. ft.
- First Floor: 1067 sq. ft.
- Other Floor: 800 sq. ft.
- Size: 40' x 27'
- Entry: Front
- Photos of Farmhouses on page 129.

Second Floor

Add as many windows and doors as you wish, to enjoy your view and deck living.

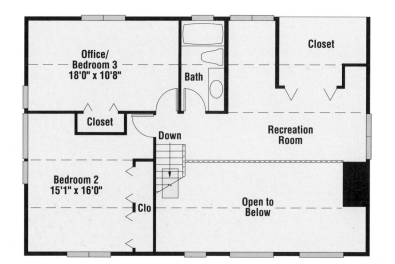

Office/
Bedroom 3
18'0" x 10'8"

Bath

Closet

Closet

Down

Bedroom 2
15'1" x 16'0"

Clo

Recreation
Room

Open to
Below

Consider optional stockade corners on round log siding for a truly rustic look.

specifications

All new homes are not created equal. Variations in the quality of building-

ing materials and specifications have become so dramatic that it's essential

to know what you're getting for your money. At Lindal, we're proud to

show you the quality that goes into your home—and why it doesn't pay to settle for anything less. In fact, "settling for less" can easily wind

up costing more in the long run. So here are the nuts and bolts of our

legendary quality—the advantages, large and small, that make a living

difference every day, for as long as you own your Lindal.

Cedar: A Natural Wonder

The Lindal difference begins with nature's most perfect building material—Western red cedar. The enduring beauty of our fragrant, fine-grained wood is visible in its natural radiance, warm range of colors and velvety finish—all of which make it a daily luxury to live with.

But the beauty of cedar is more than skin deep; pound for pound, it's as strong as steel, with remarkable insulating properties and a natural resistance to weather, decay, pests and climatic extremes that assure a lifetime of low maintenance and high value. What's more, the quality of Lindal cedar can't be matched at the local lumber yard; the strict standards of our quality control and grading systems begin where industry standards end.

Caring for the future: through donations to Global ReLeaf America's oldest national citizen conservation organization, and other tree-planting organizations, Lindal's reforestation program funds the planting of many thousands of trees each year.

It's amazing what passes for building lumber these days. Lumber that "makes the grade" today can have many more defects and weaknesses than were permitted twenty years ago. But a passing grade is not enough at Lindal; we have our own high standards for the cedar we use. Our standards start at the uppermost end of the industry's grade range. And then we visually inspect every log and piece of lumber to make sure it meets them. Lindal's "above-grade" quality control system means we reject much of the lumber that ends up in conventional stick-built homes.

Specifications are subject to change. Always consult the current general specifications sheet.

"The cedar woodwork

Under a microscope, a cross-section of cedar reveals the secret of its exceptional insulating ability: nearly ten million air-filled cells in every cubic inch. Its uniform cell structure gives cedar twelve times the insulating value of stone or concrete—and makes it easy to work with, stable against shrinking and swelling. Cedar's natural preservative oils account for its durability and resistance to moisture, decay and insects.

Cedar's visual characteristics include a flared base and thick, fibrous reddish-brown bark.

Lindal designed its own special breed of sawmill to use only small logs that meet our high criteria for quality—and our commitment to using a plentiful, renewable resource. Having our own sawmill gives us, and you, major advantages in the pricing and reliable supply of cedar in an industry plagued by uncertain availability.

The abundant use of cedar detailing is a natural with the open beauty of Lindal's post and beam construction. OR

lends warmth and a general spirit of welcome to our home." Gene and Debbie DiGiovanni, MA

A Builder Speaks Out:

"Over the past year, my company has been the general contractor for four Lindal cedar homes. The materials package Lindal homeowners receive is a reflection of materials used in a bygone era.

The norm for most new housing in Ontario is green framing material, aspenite sheathing for walls, roofs and subfloors—minimum standards that barely meet building code requirements, with design inflexibility. It's a pleasure to work with material that is straight, dry and doesn't require constant scrutiny or culling." Richard Roth, ON

By drying our cedar in our own kilns, we reduce and control the moisture content, virtually eliminating the twisting and warping that can occur in green or air-dried lumber. Kiln-drying also reduces the weight of the wood, which keeps our cedar homes a competitive value all over the world.

"Our cedar-lined ceilings are a work of art." Roberta and Doug Burrows, ON

247

The Strengths of Our System

Home to discerning buyers for over fifty years, Lindal's engineered building system is inspired by the post and beam architecture of North American masterbuilders. Rather than using conventional "stick" construction, in which the walls support the roof's weight, we use a strong framework of posts and beams, placed 5'4" on center, to carry the load. Because Lindal's interior walls are freed from serving as structural supports, the result is an open, airy interior that allows long spans, large expanses of glass—and the design flexibility to customize any floorplan to suit your functional and aesthetic tastes. The beauty and integrity of Lindal's engineered system include dozens of top-of-the-line construction details. What's more, we can customize your home's design to stand up to the snow, wind and seismic conditions of your locale.

Dear Mr. Lindal,

Hurricane Iniki's winds reached a constant 160 mph, with gusts over 180 mph. These sustained winds and extremely heavy rain continued to batter our area all day. We watched as whole roofs, porches and entire homes were destroyed. Our Lindal cedar home, with its outstanding materials and construction, had weathered the storm with no structural damage and minimal other damage. There was no wind or water leakage. We would like to thank our consultant and your company for the outstanding design work and materials which saved our home.

Pat & Jim Litchhult
Patricia and James Litchhult,
Kauai, Hawaii

Innovator and industry leader, Sir Walter Lindal holds an impressive array of U.S., Canadian and international patents for innovations that distinguish the building system, and structural integrity, of every Lindal home.

Lindal Cedar Homes is listed and complies with the standards set by the National Evaluation Service, which reviews products and systems for compliance with the three national code organizations in the United States: BOCA, ICBO and SBCCI. Most building departments have copies

of Lindal's NER-461 report on file.

In Canada, we are listed with the National Research Council Canada (CCMC 05500-R).

And in Japan, in cooperation with the Nippon Sheet Glass Company, we are listed with the Japanese Ministry of Construction.

"Post and beam construction allowed us to visually expand our home by eliminating load-bearing walls, which is

Post and Beam vs. Stick

Although Lindal's engineered building system is sophisticated and innovative, the basic premise of post and beam is simple and ingenious: a strong framework of posts and beams carries all structural loads, including the weight of the roof.

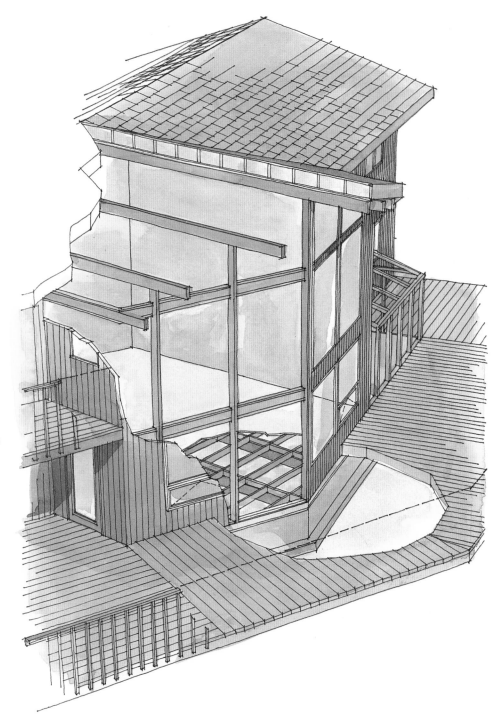

Glue-Laminated Roof and Loft Beams.
Built of kiln-dried Douglas fir/Western larch, our architectural grade, glue-laminated beams do not split, warp or twist the way solid wood beams can. They're structurally more sound too.

Supporting Posts.
The roof's weight is supported by sturdy posts and beams, rather than the partitions on which conventional construction depends. Exposed posts are glue-laminated to prevent splitting and to assure a lifetime of good looks.

A Superior Floor System.
Lindal's post and beam system starts with a strong, rigid floor that stays that way. We place our floor beams closer together—5'4" on-center; top them with 2x6 joists and then glue and screw the subfloor of ¾" tongue and groove plywood to the joists. Lindal floors are virtually immune to the squeaks and bounces of so many floors today.

Non-Load-Bearing Interior Partitions
make for flexible design. Conventionally framed.

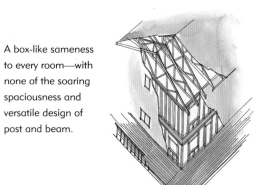

Stick:
With a conventional "stick" house, design is limited by load-bearing interior walls; the truss roof means flat ceilings, too. The result?

A box-like sameness to every room—with none of the soaring spaciousness and versatile design of post and beam.

not possible in stick construction." Homeowner, NC

249

When it comes to the differences that distinguish a Lindal home, our top-quality cedar and strong building system are only the beginning. A whole houseful of above-grade specifications are the secret to a Lindal's dramatic beauty, structural integrity, low maintenance and lasting value. If you've done a little shopping around, you may have been told that you can get the same impeccable quality for a lower bottom line. But are you getting the information you need to make an apples-to-apples comparison? Here's a look at how dramatically our Lindal specifications differ from the bulk of today's "quality" custom homes—and why the Lindal difference makes a difference to you.

The Lindal Difference

Siding

Why does so much wood siding come in such short lengths? Because so many defects have to be cut out of today's wood to make it usable. Even so, siding with loose or missing knots (which cause air leaks) still gets by. But Lindal starts with select, tight-knot Western red cedar—a grade that makes for long, beautiful siding. Because it has no loose or missing knots and fewer butt joints (where one piece of siding meets another), it's more energy efficient, too.

Framing Lumber

Much of the framing lumber that passes industry grading doesn't make the grade at Lindal. Industry standards for "on grade" lumber actually permit wane in which up to one-third the thickness and one-third the width of the full length of the board can be missing. Lindal's stringent visual re-grading system greatly reduces the amount of wane, cupping and splitting.

Beams

Did you know that a new home's most important structural members can actually be fill grade—allowing surface and internal gouges as long as eighteen inches and as deep as 1½"? Lindal specifies premium architectural grade glue-laminated beams of Douglas fir/ Western larch. (All exposed posts are glue-laminated, too.) And our visual inspection keeps them at the highest end of this higher grade—with no internal gouges and only minor surface fills. All beams come to you wrapped for protection.

Plywood

Many new homes use 3-ply plywood sheathing for their floors, walls and roofs. Lindal uses 4, 5 and 7 ply, which is much more stable, and easier to work with. Just as important, we sheath the entire house with it, while many of today's conventional homes use it only at the corners—or nowhere at all. OR

"We refer to our home as being built like the Rock of Gibraltar." Stanley and Lois Grant, NH

When you compare prices, be sure to compare quality. Ask any and all competitive bidders to base their prices on Lindal's standard materials—same quality (when they can get it), same quantity. Year in, year out, our homeowners tell us they got more home for their money. Value is the Lindal difference.

MATERIALS CHECK LIST

☐ Siding/kiln-dried cedar
☐ Upgraded framing
☐ Clear cedar windows
☐ Low E Glass
☐ Cedar soffits
☐ 4, 5 & 7 ply plywood
☐ Cedar ___

Windows
Our deep-silled, clear-cedar framed windows are not only beautiful; they're much more energy efficient than the aluminum- and vinyl-framed windows so common in new homes. And Lindal windows come with Low E Argon glass standard. CT

Others' Options Are Our Standards
From Tyvek® housewrap and 25-year roof shingles to clear cedar baseboard and top residential hardware, the quality details that cost extra in most new homes are standard with every Lindal home.

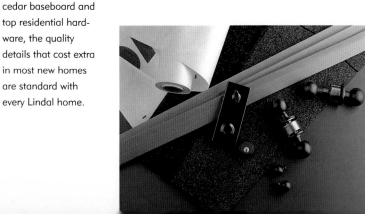

Soffits/Overhangs
When you gaze out of your new home, will you see soffits of plywood or hardboard—or long-lasting, tongue and groove wood soffits that complement the rest of the finely finished wood throughout your Lindal?

Doors
Most of today's interior passage doors are hollow—flimsy to the touch and sadly lacking as sound barriers. The solid feel and sound absorption of a solid-core interior door is one more sign of Lindal quality.

Decks
Bouncy, squeaky decks, built of 1"-thick decking, are common even in custom homes. But Lindal decks are strong and silent, thanks to our select, tight knot 2x4 or 2x6 cedar decking and 2x8 undercarriage— the best in the industry. What's more, our decking is finished on all four sides, with rounded edges to prevent splintering.

Cedar Frame Homes

Lindal's Cedar Frame home is double-wall, or cavity, construction with cedar siding on the exterior. Between the outer and inner walls are Tyvek® housewrap, plywood sheathing and—what's most important— two layers of insulation. The inside layer actually overlaps the framing itself, eliminating the customary gaps in insulation. Inside, on the warm side, the second layer of insulation is sealed with a vapor barrier. It all adds up to a home that's strong, quiet, well-insulated and built to last. And you can choose from three styles of exterior siding to get just the look you want.

Lindal's Two Building Systems

Lindal offers two major building systems: our Cedar Frame homes shown here and our Solid Cedar homes shown on pages 254 and 255. Your choice will probably have as much to do with your personal taste as anything. Whichever you prefer, you can count on the same quality cedar, the same post and beam construction—and the above-grade specifications that make every Lindal a veritable fortress of lasting strength, high energy efficiency and low maintenance.

• All three styles of Lindal exterior siding are kiln-dried, select-grade Western red cedar. Interior partitions can be lined with optional cedar liner.

• Lindal's standard wall system is 6¼" thick and has a high R-value of 22.

• The house is literally wrapped with Tyvek® housewrap, which dramatically reduces air infiltration and heat loss while letting moisture pass through to prevent condensation in the walls.

• If you live in an extremely cold region, we recommend the optional Polar Wall —8¾" thick with an R-value of 28.

• Add insulation to your roof first. Because more heat escapes out of the roof than the walls of a home, it's the best place to add extra insulation. It's not costly to add more when you build—but it's an expensive hassle later on.

• A frame, or "cavity" roof system is standard with Lindal Cedar Frame homes. Filled with fiberglass batt insulation, it has a top R-33 value rating. Premium cedar ceiling liner is a popular option.

Note: you can substitute a rigid insulation roof for the frame roof.

What R and U-Values Mean to You

The insulating ability of a home's walls, roof, floors and doors is measured in terms of R-value. Windows, however, are rated in terms of U-values. And just to make things complicated, R and U-values are inversely related; the higher the R-values and the lower the U-values, the better.

All R and U-values are based on the American Society of Heating, Refrigeration and Air Conditioning Engineers, Inc. (ASHRAE) Handbook of Fundamentals. R-values in Canada are calculated differently and vary slightly from the U.S. values given here. As government and industry standards are constantly changing, check with your Lindal consultant for current R and U-values.

"We have compared the Lindal method of construction with that of other houses

Choose Your Favorite Cedar Frame Siding: Classic: vertical tongue and groove cedar siding.

Clapboard: horizontal overlapping cedar siding. Also known as bevel siding.

Round Log: 8" horizontal tongue and groove cedar log rounds. Optional stockade corners.

Cedar Frame Roof System: R-33

Composite shingles.

Building paper.

½" plywood sheathing.

R-30 fiberglass insulation.

2x12 rafters; 24" on-center.

Continuous vapor barrier.

Optional cedar liner or drywall inside.

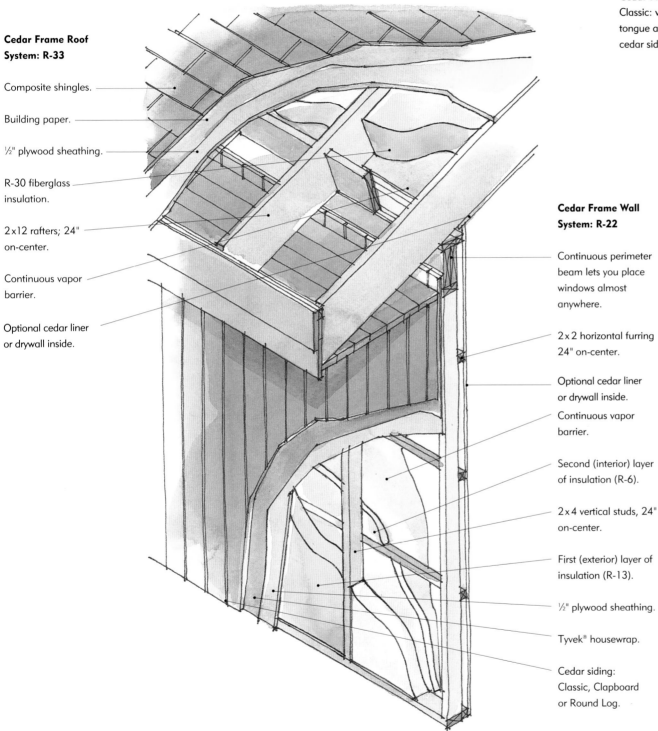

Cedar Frame Wall System: R-22

Continuous perimeter beam lets you place windows almost anywhere.

2x2 horizontal furring 24" on-center.

Optional cedar liner or drywall inside.

Continuous vapor barrier.

Second (interior) layer of insulation (R-6).

2x4 vertical studs, 24" on-center.

First (exterior) layer of insulation (R-13).

½" plywood sheathing.

Tyvek® housewrap.

Cedar siding: Classic, Clapboard or Round Log.

Polar Options for Extreme Climates

Lindal Polar Cap I Roof—R-41
Added high-density insulation for cold climates. Trus Joist MacMillan® I-Beam Roof.

Lindal Polar Cap II Roof—Up to R-63
Two layers of R-30 insulation for severely cold regions. Expandable E Rafter Roof to 22" cavity.

Lindal Polar Wall— R-28
An 8¾"-thick insulated wall for extremely cold regions.

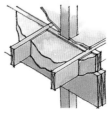

Lindal Polar Floor— R-21
Ideal for Lindals built in cold climates over a crawl space instead of a full basement.

being custom-built in our neighborhood, and we are glad we chose Lindal." Derek and Candy Stott, ON

We've set a new standard in the strength, sophistication and energy efficiency of log homes. Crafted of 4×8 finely finished solid cedar

Solid Cedar Homes

timbers, the walls of Lindal Solid Cedar homes are edged with double tongues and grooves that lock together for an airtight, zero-tolerance fit. The principle of "thermal mass" also contributes to a level of energy efficiency that rivals frame homes with high R-values; the solid cedar walls store heat during warm weather and time-release it slowly and evenly as temperatures drop.

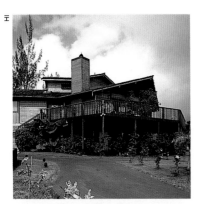

• Kiln-dried cedar contributes to dimensional stability, airtight fit and energy efficiency. Unlike most log homes, no straps, cables, tie rods or bolts are needed to hold ours together.

• The solid cedar, airtight Energy Lock Wall eliminates the draftiness and settling typical of log homes. In fact, the fit is so precise that no caulking is required between timbers.

• At intersecting walls, the optimum woodworking joint—the dovetail—is used to prevent movement and slippage.

• Because we pre-cut the timbers for each home and label each one for course (layer) and location, construction is fast and easy.

• Interior partitions can be lined with optional cedar or drywall.

• A 2×6 double tongued and grooved plank roof with 5" of solid insulation provides excellent energy efficiency and a high R-38 value rating. And it gives you the interior warmth and beauty of a lustrous wood ceiling.

• The Lindal solid cedar home is a proud successor to the Justus solid cedar home. New name, same exceptional building system.

Note: you can substitute a frame roof for the rigid insulation or vice versa.

Ample Ventilation
Whatever Lindal cavity roof system you choose, you can count on excellent ventilation—thanks to a continuous soffit vent and a ridge vent that runs the entire length of the soffit and ridge. Together, they create a continuous air flow that keeps roof framing and insulation dry, preventing the moisture that can cause rot and mold. Our roof ventilation system also channels out unwanted heat in summer, which can save on air conditioning.

Tropical Specifications
Lindal's tropical specifications eliminate unneeded insulation, make the most of ventilation—and take advantage of cedar's natural resistance to insects and decay. For details, ask your local Lindal consultant for our Tradewinds planbook and specification sheet.

"Our previous home was a well-insulated brick home, only ten years old. Our Lindal solid cedar home is easier to heat and cool than the

**Solid Cedar
Rigid Insulation Roof
System: R-38**

Composite shingles.

Building paper.

½" plywood sheathing.

4" of solid foam ther-
mal insulation plus 1"
of styrene (R-33).

2×8 rafters, 24"
on-center.

2×6 double tongue
and groove solid-
wood planks.

**Solid Cedar
Energy Lock Wall**

Top timber acts as a
continuous perimeter
beam for flexible
placement of windows.

Diagonal cuts wedge
timbers tight to pre-
vent shearing, racking
and lateral pressure.

Second diagonal
jog provides added
defense against
weather.

Solid 4×8 double
tongue and groove
cedar timbers.

Note: cedar does not
penetrate through to
the outside at wall
intersections—for
superior protection
against weather and
air infiltration.

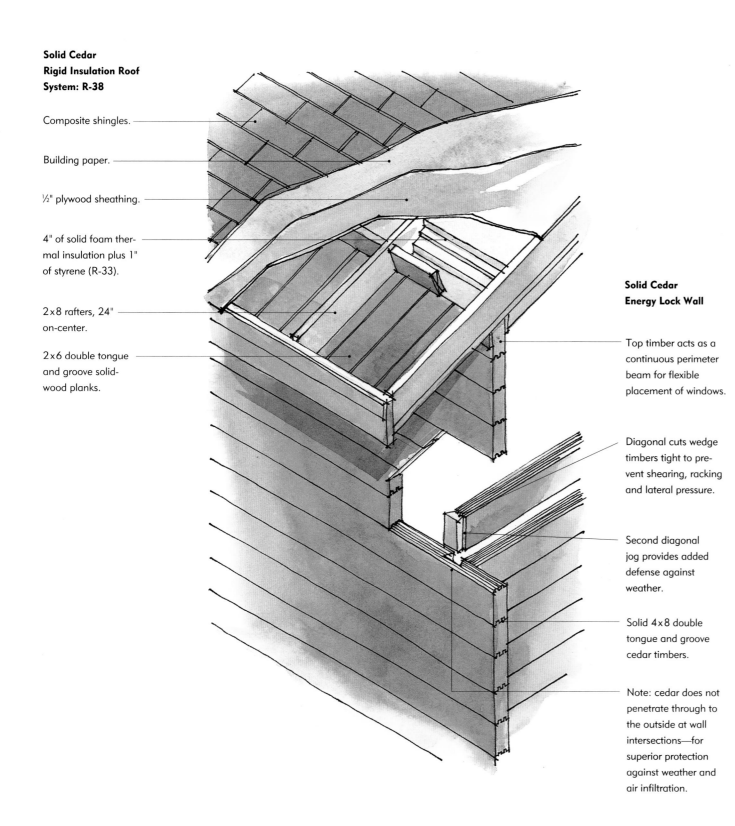

previous home of equal size." Calvin and Connie Johnson, IL

Solid cedar fascia
graces eaves and
gables.

Composite shingles
with a 25-year guar-
antee are standard.
Premium composite
upgrades are optional.

Thick-butt, handsplit,
resawn No. 1 grade
cedar shakes are a
deluxe option.

Lindal Windows

Every Lindal window is framed like fine furniture—in such clear, fine-grained Western red cedar that it's a view in itself; no need to cover it up with vinyl. And when you look beyond its sheer beauty, you'll find the highest industry rating available for its ability to prevent air and water infiltration under maximum test conditions. But any window can be a major source of energy loss. So it pays to know what you can do to boost insulation. Lindal starts with state-of-the-art Low E Argon glass windows as our standard. Besides having excellent U-values, Low E Argon also reduces fading of draperies and furniture fabrics.

Glass Options
Glazing technology gets better all the time; check with your Lindal consultant for the latest options and local building code requirements.

Low E Argon Glass Standard
This transparent coating lets short wavelength sunlight enter your home and keeps it there by reflecting it back into the room. In hot weather, Low E also reduces heat gain by reflecting long wavelength heat rays.

Argon gas fills the space between the two panels. This inert, colorless, non-corroding and non-reactive gas is completely safe and increases energy performance significantly.

Heat Mirror® Glass Optional
This layer of transparent polyester film, with a heat-reflective coating, is stretched tight between the two panes of glass, creating two air spaces.

Fiberglass screens are standard with all Lindal opening windows.

Low E Argon glass reduces heat loss, drafts, noise and condensation build-up as well as offering outstanding energy efficiency.

A variety of glazing options are available: single glazed, double glazed, Low E and Heat Mirror®. Also: clear, obscure and tinted.

Top-quality window hardware with gear crank handle for smooth, effortless operation.

Mortise and tenon joints are used for the wood joints of our casement and awning windows to give an airtight, watertight fit.

Lindal's clear cedar window frames don't sweat like aluminum (which also conducts heat out an amazing 2,000 times faster than wood). Optional fir frames give a thinner profile.

Two strips of continuous weather-stripping (much like a refrigerator) stop air infiltration and reduce drafts.

Note: Lindal window styles are shown on page 151.

"The large, Low E glass windows afford plenty of light and wonderful views of the outside—yet don't allow transfer of cold air." Ian and Holly Green, CT

Lindal Floors

Over the years, your floor will get more wear and tear than any other part of your home. So it's good to know that Lindal floors are built to stand up to a lifetime of everyday use—without getting loose or squeaky along the way. It's just one more Lindal difference.

How Much Floor Insulation?

• The answer depends on your climate, local building codes and what you're building over: a crawl space, basement, post and pier, concrete slab or permanent wood foundation.

• If you're building over crawl spaces in a cold climate, consider a Polar Floor (R-21). But if you're building over a basement, you don't need the extra insulation. Instead, consider adding an inch or more of rigid insulation to line the exterior of your basement walls, bringing them up to an R-value of 5 or more.

• Another possibility: a permanent wood foundation with R-values of 20 to 30. It is strong, long-lasting and easily brought into sites that are difficult for concrete trucks to reach. And the same crew that builds your house can do the foundation.

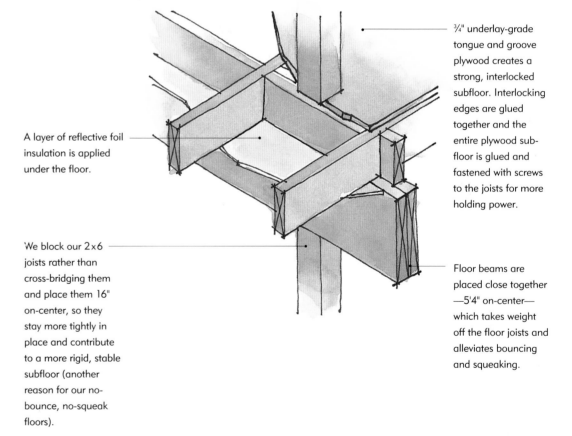

¾" underlay-grade tongue and groove plywood creates a strong, interlocked subfloor. Interlocking edges are glued together and the entire plywood sub-floor is glued and fastened with screws to the joists for more holding power.

A layer of reflective foil insulation is applied under the floor.

We block our 2×6 joists rather than cross-bridging them and place them 16" on-center, so they stay more tightly in place and contribute to a more rigid, stable subfloor (another reason for our no-bounce, no-squeak floors).

Floor beams are placed close together —5'4" on-center— which takes weight off the floor joists and alleviates bouncing and squeaking.

"With Low E windows and the Polar Floor option, during the past two winters our monthly electric bill was less than half that of other comparable homes." Homeowners, OR

Lindal Doors

The doors in your home are a highly personal choice—and it's not at all unusual for style to be a primary concern, especially at the main entrance. But think about security and energy efficiency as well as good looks; we have. That's why Lindal's standard entry door is made of galvanized steel with a polyurethane core, and our handsome wood door is optional. Our interior doors give you the strength and noise insulation of solid wood. And our glass doors make magical transitions between rooms or from the inside out; their wood frames act as a natural insulator— with double glazing, airtight weather-stripping and a thermal break.

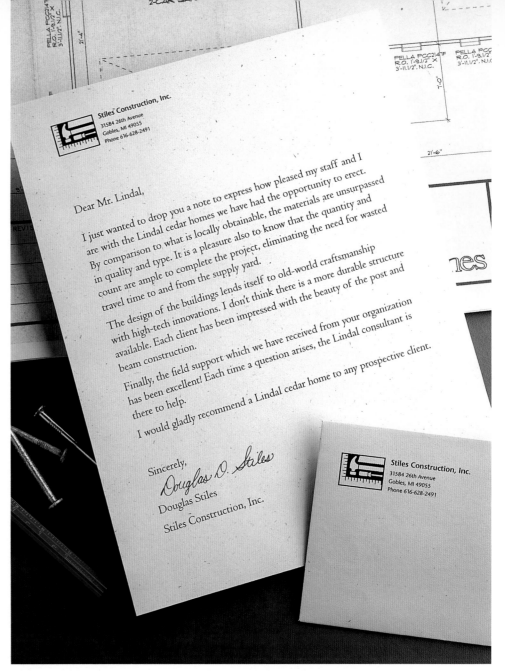

A builder speaks out.

Standard 24-gauge
galvanized steel
entry door.

Optional raised panel
solid wood entry door.

"Lindal windows and doors are very high quality and not only finish well— but also do a wonderful job of sealing out the weather." Builder: David J. Howard, Howard Homes, MI

Lindal Delivers

You can be promised all the high-quality materials in the world, but if that promise isn't delivered on in a complete and timely fashion, it can cost you a lot of time and money. So it's not just the quality of Lindal's building materials and specifications that distinguishes every one of our homes. It's our willingness to guarantee that you'll have what you need—when you need it—to build your dream. When we say "Lindal delivers," here's what it means to you:

• Superior building materials most of which you just can't find anywhere else.
• Sixty-day price protection to take delivery from the time you sign on the dotted line.
• Our guarantee that everything in your Lindal package will arrive on time and in one delivery (or more, if desirable)—so there's no downtime and no "windshield time" spent driving to the local hardware store.
• Our guarantee that you'll receive enough materials to build your home without material cost overruns on all Lindal components—an amazingly rare guarantee in our industry.

• The assistance of your Lindal dealership in analyzing your site and providing custom design services through pricing, ordering, delivery, inventory and follow-up services long after your home is complete.

Critical building components are part-numbered for easy reference to your blueprints and materials list. And the floor system, wall planks and roof boards are tongued and grooved for easy assembly.

Your final Lindal building materials list is computerized and cross-referenced to your final blueprints.

how to get your original

The pleasures of transforming your dream into your Lindal original are

as close as your local Lindal consultant—and chances are that's not far

from where you are right now. That's because our homes are sold through

the largest, most experienced network of independent dealerships in North America. According to our homeowners, this supportive, collaborative

relationship is absolutely key to making your dream home come true. And

all it takes to get started is a visit to your local Lindal consultant, who

will help you create the most exciting cedar home in the world. Your own.

Throughout this book, you've read the stories of many Lindal home-owners, and you've seen the homes we've helped them create—homes as unique as the individuals and the dreams that inspired them. Yet for all

"I Love My Lindal"

of their one-of-a-kind character, Lindal homes share some important strengths that dramatically distinguish them from the crowd of "custom" homes and lead to the lasting delight of dreams come true. Time and again, here's what homeowners say they love about their Lindal cedar homes—day after day, year after year:

"I plan to live here until I'm 101." Trudy Powelson, NJ

"Living in our Lindal is like being on

"I love the feeling of the outside coming in. I even refer to the bedroom loft as my treehouse." Debbie & Ken Wilson, NC

Original by design.
Lindal gives you the design flexibility, expertise and support to turn your wish list into your dream home.

Lasting beauty.
The open, airy designs of post and beam construction, the warm glow of Western red cedar, and the craftsmanship in every detail surround you with a timeless beauty that's an enduring source of pleasure and pride.

Energy efficiency in any climate.
The more precious and expensive energy sources become, the more homeowners appreciate their Lindal's ability to stay cost-effectively cool in warm weather, warm and snug in cold weather.

Local know-how.
With hundreds of independent Lindal dealerships throughout North America and the world, the assistance you need is close at hand.

Quality and value for life.
At a time when shortcuts are common in the homebuilding industry, Lindal homeowners say our unwavering standards of quality are a rare and welcome exception.

"Our local consultants were more than helpful. Their support,

advice, information, communication and friendship made it an exciting

and joyful time, especially since we were 500 miles from the site." Don and Carole Forbes, VA

vacation every day." David and Cathy Osterman, TN

The Dusek Family, WA

Deer Parks Journal

DECEMBER

How lucky can we be—a beautiful Lindal
in a fairytale setting. The deer roam freely;
nearly every day we have visitors. Georgia
has them eating out of her hand. They bring
their new babies to meet her. Although her
father called our land the Hog Ranch
(because of all the mud when we first saw it)
and the carpenters called it Overkill Acres
(because everything was built to exceed
minimum code), Georgia wants to
call it Deer Parks. How fitting!

Sherman

A sure thing.
From pinning down all the
planning details to delivering a
complete, part-coded building
package to your site, we've spent
50 years taking the uncertainties
out of building a custom home.
In the building industry, Lindal's
type of reliability is one of the
rarest commodities of all.

Here today, here tomorrow.
Lindal has the longstanding
strength and stability you want
from a company when you're
making one of life's biggest invest-
ments. The result is an original
that stands the test of time—
from a company that does, too.

"The warmth of cedar, combined with flexible design,

has been the answer to our dream home." Elouise Brown, OR

263

As a publicly held company and the world's largest manufacturer of custom cedar homes, Lindal's size and financial strength let us pass volume discounts on to you; control quality from forest to building site; and develop new products that make your Lindal a growing pleasure to live in.

Dream homes don't happen by chance. They take careful planning, coordination and attention to detail. And the success of the end result is directly related to the quality of the team involved. At Lindal, your team combines the best of both worlds: the hands-on advice and attention of

Your Dream Team

your local consultant—with the experience, financial strength and quality assurance of a company that stands behind you, from start to finish, and long afterwards, too. This is the kind of teamwork it takes to turn a dream into a living reality. Ultimately, it's the secret of our success, and—most important of all— your satisfaction.

Your Lindal consultant will help analyze your plans for site suitability, functionality and aesthetics— and suggest means and ways to build your dream within your budget.

A visit to your local consultant's model home or Lindal Design Center is the best way to experience the Lindal difference firsthand.

1-800-426-0536

Where to begin? *By now you probably know the name and location of your Lindal consultant. If not, call us toll-free at 1-800-426-0536. Because your local independent Lindal dealership is where you'll find the advice and support you need to build your dream. Stop by for a visit, and when you do, be sure to ask for a Home Planning Kit. It's brimming with information and tools that make it easy—and exciting—to transform your dream into scale drawings of the real thing.*

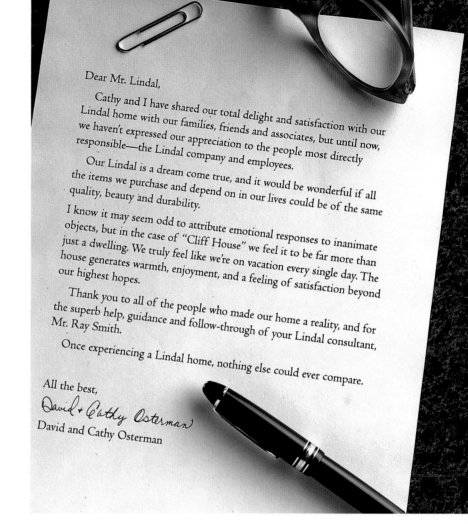

Dear Mr. Lindal,

Cathy and I have shared our total delight and satisfaction with our Lindal home with our families, friends and associates, but until now, we haven't expressed our appreciation to the people most directly responsible—the Lindal company and employees.

Our Lindal is a dream come true, and it would be wonderful if all the items we purchase and depend on in our lives could be of the same quality, beauty and durability.

I know it may seem odd to attribute emotional responses to inanimate objects, but in the case of "Cliff House" we feel it to be far more than just a dwelling. We truly feel like we're on vacation every single day. The house generates warmth, enjoyment, and a feeling of satisfaction beyond our highest hopes.

Thank you to all of the people who made our home a reality, and for the superb help, guidance and follow-through of your Lindal consultant, Mr. Ray Smith.

Once experiencing a Lindal home, nothing else could ever compare.

All the best,

David + Cathy Osterman
David and Cathy Osterman

Getting the Home Planning Kit at your local participating dealership is the next step towards your own original.

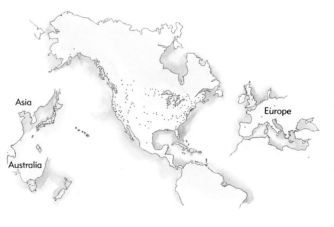

Asia

Europe

Australia

We realize the importance of the relationship between local support and satisfied customers. Hundreds of dealers across North America and throughout the world—trained at Lindal University and honoring a Code of Ethics—are awaiting the opportunity to serve you.

Cedar's fresh, clean scent - so evocative of its wilderness roots - provides daily aromatherapy for heart and home.

While the talk in today's boardrooms is all about how to revive quality,

we're proud to announce that it's alive and well in every Lindal cedar

home. In fact, it's been the foundation of our company, and our homes, # From Our Family to Yours

for half a century. And it always will be. But we not only give you our word; we give you our ten-year

guarantee—the best in the industry. After all, when you're building the

dream of a lifetime, you should be able to count on a happy ending.

Sir Walter Lindal is
the founder of Lindal
Cedar Homes and its
50-year reputation
for excellence. His
four children (left to
right: Doug, Bonnie,
Bob and Marty) are
actively involved
in the company's
daily management;
Robert Lindal has
been President and
CEO since 1981.

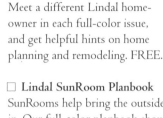

Your Free Lindal Dream Home Planning Kit

Gift Certificate

Simply bring this gift certificate to your local *participating* Lindal dealership to receive all the indispensable planning tools and professional tips in your free Lindal Home Planning Kit. And be sure to complete the following information:

```
   L469552   PLB4 X     5
Ms. Carol Brohard
385 Adobe Ln
Tracy, CA  95376
```

Independently distributed by:

Telephone _____

Location of Building Property _____

_____

For the name of your nearest Lindal dealer call 1-800-426-0536.

⌂ Lindal Cedar Homes

Please rush me the information checked on reverse side.

Method of payment:
- ☐ Check   ☐ VISA   ☐ MasterCard
- ☐ Discover

Card Number _____

Expiration Date _____

Signature _____
(required for credit card orders)

Name _____

Address _____

_____

Telephone _____

⌂ Lindal Cedar Homes
1-800-426-0536

We need your help.

We are constantly searching for ways to better serve you, and would appreciate your taking a minute to complete the survey below:

1. Do you own a building lot?   ☐ Yes   ☐ No

2. Where did you purchase or see a Lindal planbook?
   - ☐ Dealer   ☐ Lindal   ☐ Bookstore
   - ☐ Friend   ☐ Other_____

3. Would you like to receive the name of your nearest Lindal dealer?   ☐ Yes   ☐ No

Thank you for your assistance.

To order call 1-800-426-0536 or mail to:

UNITED STATES
Lindal Cedar Homes
P. O. Box 24426, Dept. PBI
Seattle, WA 98124

CANADA
Lindal Cedar Homes
10880 Dyke Road, Dept. PBI
Surrey, B.C. V3V 7P4

Please rush me the information checked on reverse side.

Method of payment:
- ☐ Check   ☐ VISA   ☐ MasterCard
- ☐ Discover

Card Number _____

Expiration Date _____

Signature _____
(required for credit card orders)

Name _____

Address _____

_____

Telephone _____

⌂ Lindal Cedar Homes
1-800-426-0536

We need your help.

We are constantly searching for ways to better serve you, and would appreciate your taking a minute to complete the survey below:

1. Do you own a building lot?   ☐ Yes   ☐ No

2. Where did you purchase or see a Lindal planbook?
   - ☐ Dealer   ☐ Lindal   ☐ Bookstore
   - ☐ Friend   ☐ Other_____

3. Would you like to receive the name of your nearest Lindal dealer?   ☐ Yes   ☐ No

Thank you for your assistance.

To order call 1-800-426-0536 or mail to:

UNITED STATES
Lindal Cedar Homes
P. O. Box 24426, Dept. PBI
Seattle, WA 98124

CANADA
Lindal Cedar Homes
10880 Dyke Road, Dept. PBI
Surrey, B.C. V3V 7P4

Please rush me the information checked on reverse side.

Method of payment:
- ☐ Check   ☐ VISA   ☐ MasterCard
- ☐ Discover

Card Number _____

Expiration Date _____

Signature _____
(required for credit card orders)

Name _____

Address _____

_____

Telephone _____

⌂ Lindal Cedar Homes
1-800-426-0536

We need your help.

We are constantly searching for ways to better serve you, and would appreciate your taking a minute to complete the survey below:

1. Do you own a building lot?   ☐ Yes   ☐ No

2. Where did you purchase or see a Lindal planbook?
   - ☐ Dealer   ☐ Lindal   ☐ Bookstore
   - ☐ Friend   ☐ Other_____

3. Would you like to receive the name of your nearest Lindal dealer?   ☐ Yes   ☐ No

Thank you for your assistance.

To order call 1-800-426-0536 or mail to:

UNITED STATES
Lindal Cedar Homes
P. O. Box 24426, Dept. PBI
Seattle, WA 98124

CANADA
Lindal Cedar Homes
10880 Dyke Road, Dept. PBI
Surrey, B.C. V3V 7P4

Lindal Cedar Homes

UNITED STATES
4300 South 104th Place
P. O. Box 24426
Seattle, Washington 98124
Phone: (206) 725-0900

CANADA
10880 Dyke Road
Surrey, British Columbia
V3V 7P4
Phone: (604) 580-1191

Toll-free Phone 1-800-426-0536

Printed in Japan Copyright 1994 by Lindal Cedar Homes, Inc.

Case Residence, VA